PRAISE FOR *DESIGN ANY DISASTER*

"Patrick Hardy has written a book full of sound, practical wisdom, beginning from the standpoint that disasters are quite literally what you make them by your action or inaction. He has a gift for boiling down complex truths into simple, actionable maxims that can guide professional emergency managers as much as individual employees or private citizens. Highly recommended reading for anyone who needs to build the ability to survive and thrive in an increasingly eventful world—in other words, for all of us."

—Dr. Peter Williams, strategy consultant and chair at ARISE-US

"*Design Any Disaster* is a must-read for people of all walks of life. A book that will open your mind and allow you to take control of your own fate. It contains useful and enlightening information about disaster preparedness that anyone can put into action. Patrick Hardy perfectly illustrates the concept that you can easily prepare to be your own first responder."

—Cheryl Nelson, meteorologist and founder and owner of Prepare with Cher, LLC

"What an outstanding, practical read, and incredible resource guide for the average family just trying to protect themselves in this modern complex threat environment. Patrick Hardy's C³ Method breaks down the emergency planning cycle into its simplest form, and provides core recommendations on how to mitigate and prepare for even the most complex incidents. Whether you're a seasoned emergency manager, or an average person just trying to protect their family, this is the book and resource guide for you . . . I would highly encourage purchasing this wonderful book."

—Lester J. Millet III, executive director of InfraGard Louisiana Members Alliance

"*Design Any Disaster* will be required reading for many years to come. This is a superb book that empowers readers to prepare for disasters by taking command, communicating, and working together during and after disasters. Practical approach for families, small businesses to everyone in the community."

—Teresa Cox, Fremont City councilmember

DESIGN ANY DISASTER

DESIGN ANY DISASTER

**The Revolutionary Blueprint to Master
Your Next Crisis or Emergency**

PATRICK HARDY

BenBella Books, Inc.
Dallas, TX

Design Any Disaster copyright © 2023 by Hytropy, Inc.

BENBELLA

BenBella Books, Inc.
10440 N. Central Expressway
Suite 800
Dallas, TX 75231
benbellabooks.com
Send feedback to feedback@benbellabooks.com

BenBella is a federally registered trademark.

Hytropy Disaster Management and *Disaster Hawk*® are federally registered trademarks.

Printed in the United States of America
10 9 8 7 6 5 4 3 2 1

Library of Congress Control Number: 2022038262
ISBN 9781637742730 (print)
ISBN 9781637742747 (ebook)

Editing by Greg Brown
Copyediting by Lydia Choi
Proofreading by Kellie Doherty and Ariel Fagiola
Indexing by WordCo Indexing Services
Text design and composition by Aaron Edmiston
Cover design by Sarah Avinger
Cover photo illustration by Pete Garceau
Author photo by Mayumi Acosta
Printed by Lake Book Manufacturing

This book is dedicated to all those who live in the "Age of Disasters"

. . . You got this.

CONTENTS

PART FOUR—RECOVER: RESTORE YOUR LIFE IN FIVE SENTENCES USING THE C3 METHOD

PART FIVE—REVERSE: TRANSFORM DISASTER INTO OPPORTUNITY WITH THE C3 METHOD

A DISASTER IS ONLY A DISASTER IF YOU LET IT BE ONE!

When I was a young boy, my father took my brother and me to Universal Studios Hollywood. We experienced two "disasters" that day. The first was when I had forgotten my shoes and my dad had to purchase a pair of adult sandals at the park and reengineer them to fit the feet of a ten-year-old (with the help of a clerk at the store), and the second was when we took the famous "Studio Tour" ride, which takes passengers through multiple movie-set areas, like the ones for *Jaws* and *Back to the Future*.

At one point, the ride goes into a subway. Suddenly, there's shaking, and the earth caves in. Water rushes down the stairs, what looks like an oil tanker comes crashing in from the ceiling, and the tour guide pretends like it's all real. Then, after a minute or two, the guide gives the "just kidding," and everything returns to normal as you exit the subway and continue the tour.

My heart was beating fast for a while, as this came totally without warning—and before the time of online spoilers. Even my brother, who has some kind of daredevil gene in him and was never afraid of rides of any kind, had a startled look on his face when we emerged into the sunshine. Of course, that's the purpose of the ride: to scare you. It's supposed to simulate the real thing. We were never in danger, but we still got to experience an earthquake.

Notice that I didn't say "disaster." We simply let it happen to us, but it had no real, long-lasting effect because it was only a ride.

The reason I am telling you this story is because this is how I want you to totally change your perspective on disasters. The reason we experience disasters as horrible is not because of their size or scope. It's because we hand control of the way we react to, respond to, and recover from them to someone else. I want you to turn every disaster you face into a ride at Universal Studios. Watch it happen, then move on.

I am here to tell you that you can *Design Any Disaster*. You can put yourself in a position where you can design precisely how a disaster is going to affect you.

OVERVIEW OF DISASTERS

The fact is that disasters are everywhere. I don't have to tell you that; there's no doubt about it. In 2020, for example, there were twenty-two separate billion-dollar natural disasters involving the weather across the United States, breaking the previous annual record of sixteen events in 2017 and 2011.[1] You read about them every day. In fact, as I wrote this chapter in October 2022, the headlines today consisted of serious cyberattacks conducted at multiple US airports; the largest-ever power outage in the world in Bangladesh, affecting 140 million people; and the aftermath in Florida of Category 4 Hurricane Ian, which made landfall in September.

All disasters fit into one of three categories: natural, technological, and security. Each of these categories has unique characteristics and challenges associated with it.

NATURAL DISASTERS
Natural disasters are ones caused by the natural environment, like hurricanes, earthquakes, volcanic eruptions, and tsunamis. The increasingly visible effects of climate change have created an increased focus on natural disasters, as they have made them more frequent and more intense. For example, the California August Complex fire in 2020 burned an area larger than Rhode Island.[2] Hurricanes have also become much more destructive. Hurricane Harvey in 2017 was the most destructive storm in Texas history, causing $20 billion in damage and displacing more than 300,000 people.[3]

Natural disasters can go from the catastrophic to the very strange, as large insect swarms and even algae-formed "red tides" can be incredibly destructive. Between 2019 and 2020, the Horn of Africa experienced some of the worst insect swarms in modern history, with a single swarm of locusts growing to be about twenty-five miles long and thirty-seven miles wide, which would cover the geographic area of Paris twenty-four times over! During that period, they caused significant crop damage and food shortages.[4] The previous large locust outbreak, which began in 2003 and lasted until 2005, caused an estimated $2.5 billion in crop damage.[5]

TECHNOLOGICAL DISASTERS

Technological disasters are those that are human made but are generally either accidents or caused by negligent human behavior. Examples of these are chemical spills, bridge collapses, and utility outages. They range from the serious to the comedic. For instance, one night, a client called my company's emergency line at two o'clock in the morning, telling us there was a disaster in their RV park. When my employee asked them what the emergency was, the client stated that the internet was out. The employee asked how that was an emergency, and the client said, "I have twenty people right now trying to stream the final episode of *Game of Thrones*. Trust me, this is an emergency."

However, utility outages are common and can be quite serious. In 2017, Cape Town, South Africa, was on the verge of a serious emergency because of its declining dam levels. Local newspapers counted down the days to "Day Zero," the day the city would run out of water.[6] Electricity shortages (particularly in areas where there are high-heat days) can also have a major impact on public health. For those on constant oxygen or reliant on portable medical equipment, a long-term outage can be fatal.

Transportation accidents like airplane crashes, train derailments, or even massive traffic jams can be considered technological disasters. For instance, in July 2014, Los Angeles was conducting planned construction on the 405 Freeway, a major thoroughfare snaking through Southern California. About 300,000 cars pass through it on a typical summer weekend, and it is the major artery to the Los Angeles International Airport. City officials planned to shut down a section of the freeway for two straight weekends, which, left unaddressed, could cause a transportation shutdown that would paralyze the city and strand potentially tens of thousands in their cars in ninety-degree heat. Anticipating this, the city enacted an emergency declaration for what they termed "Carmageddon." The mayor of Los Angeles stood at a press conference with first-response and emergency-management agencies, giving instructions to the community to help avoid a potentially dangerous transportation shutdown.[7]

SECURITY DISASTERS

Security emergencies are ones that have belligerent motives. They include terrorist attacks, mass shootings, cyberattacks, and acts of warfare. The September 11, 2001, attacks on the World Trade Center and the Pentagon are obvious examples of this, as are the 1995 Oklahoma City bombing and the 2008 Mumbai attacks, but there are thousands of others that occur around the world.

However, the type of incident many people in the United States are most familiar with is mass shootings. They obviously can and do occur anywhere, but when they involve schools and/or have many casualties, they tend to make national headlines. Many trace the beginning of this trend to the April 1999 Columbine High School shooting in Littleton, Colorado, but there had been significant shootings prior to this.[8] On August 20, 1986, for example, a postal employee named Patrick Sherrill shot and killed fourteen employees and injured six at the post office in Edmond, Oklahoma. As of August 2022, it stands as the deadliest workplace mass shooting in US history.[9] In addition, the 2012 massacre at Sandy Hook, the 2007 Virginia Tech spree shooting, and the 2022 shooting in Uvalde, Texas, as well as many other mass public shootings, have since highlighted the continued need to address workplace, worship-center, and school violence.[10]

Security emergencies don't necessarily have to stem from a massive event. I work with campgrounds around the country, and one of the largest security emergencies I came across in that industry occurred in San Diego, California, when around sixty people got involved in a massive drunken, gang-inspired fight, resulting in dozens of injuries to guests and staff who were trying to avoid the maelstrom.

Cyberattacks are becoming significantly more disruptive as we increasingly rely on digital infrastructure to conduct our daily lives, and they signify a security emergency that is now in greater focus. For example, in May 2022, Costa Rica declared a state of emergency when its government websites were the target of a massive ransomware attack by an organized hacking group called Conti.[11]

Other hacks, like the Sony Pictures cyberattack in 2014, which resulted in the release of private personnel information and confidential emails, can create serious personal repercussions for employees and their families.[12]

During the COVID-19 pandemic, cyberattacks against both small and large companies from malicious employees, cybercriminals, and hacktivists increased exponentially. In Switzerland alone, the number of reported attacks in June 2020 was triple that from the previous April.[13] And cyberattacks are not limited to digital infrastructure; they can have serious impacts on brick-and-mortar assets as well. The Colonial Pipeline was the subject of a massive cyberattack in 2021, resulting in significant gas disruption along the US East Coast.[14] These attacks are growing in number as well as sophistication and will likely become a permanent fixture in the disaster-threat picture.[15]

"COMMON DISASTERS"

But I want you to add one more category of disasters. I call them "common disasters." These are disasters that occur to you but don't directly affect the larger community. However, that doesn't make them any less important. These include losing a family member unexpectedly, sewer backups and natural gas breaks, acute medical emergencies, and even unforeseen incidents that occur when you are traveling. These are disasters that can have tremendous physical, psychological, and financial effects.

Today, there are unique "common disasters" that could not have happened forty years ago. For instance, in the age of social media and the internet, you can experience an acute public-relations emergency. Every week or so, social media latches onto the photo or video of someone behaving offensively or saying something to draw public ire. These displays routinely go viral and can have grave implications for the people involved—and, sometimes, their family members—such as losing their jobs, being harassed online, or even receiving death threats.

SOLVING THE PROBLEM—USING THE C3 METHOD, YOU CAN DESIGN ANY DISASTER

Shhh. I have a secret to tell you.

Not one of the "disasters" I listed above is really a disaster. Not a single one. Every incident I mentioned above—whether natural, technological, security, or "common"—is just that: an incident. They are all incidents that, unfortunately, occur in our lives, and we have little control to stop them. But here is the key: *they only transform into disasters when you allow them to destroy and paralyze you.* That's right—the only one who turns them from an incident to a disaster is *you.*

Ultimately, you must see a disaster for what it really is: *something you can conquer.* The way to do this is to decrease the one element that indicates the severity of a disaster. It's not the number of houses destroyed or the number of people evacuated from an area. It's how dependent you are on other organizations, people, and government agencies to manage the disaster for you. In other words, how much of a bystander you are in the disaster.

That's right. I can determine right now how much a disaster will negatively affect you by analyzing your dependency on others. It has nothing to do with the category size or Richter strength or tsunami wave size. It has to do with your dependence.

The more you are a bystander in your disaster response, the more severe the disaster will be. That's why I developed a system called the C3 Method that is going to revolutionize how you prepare for, respond to, and recover from a disaster. That's the value of the C3 Method: *as you decrease your dependency on others, you decrease the Bystander Effect, which decreases the effect of disasters. This is what increases your resiliency and preparedness for them.*

Most disaster books talk about recovering post-disaster back to where you were before. Let me be clear: I am not remotely interested in that. Not at all. What I want to do is reframe your thinking so that you have a clear, applicable method for making your life stronger as a result of the disaster. Once we transform from a victim to an empowered leader in any incident, we can carry that empowered state forward to meet the next disaster. If you follow what I write in this book, you will never become a victim again. You will be a stronger, more resilient person than you were before the disaster.

I have worked in disaster management at every level: government, private-sector organizations (small and large), nonprofits (animals and people), schools and higher education, and families of all socioeconomic strata. I have worked with vulnerable populations and have spoken around the world on disaster preparedness. In my nearly two decades of doing this work, I have learned a lot. And I want to share that knowledge with you. But none more than this: *there is no disaster you can't conquer.* Notice that I didn't say "survive." I want you to be able to *conquer* a disaster so that you'll be stronger and better afterward.

The reason that incidents become disasters is because we all allow them to—because we don't have a consistent framework for thinking about them. I think this is why we generally see disorganized responses to disasters. Frankly, in many cases, no one knows really what to do or when to do it. There are many reasons for this: not having a disaster plan in place, not having proper equipment beforehand, and a lack of participation in drills. But I think the real culprit for not having a consistent disaster-response framework is our expectation that someone else will take care of it. When we don't prepare, and when we don't have a framework in place to consistently respond effectively to a disaster, we are handing control over to someone else at the worst possible time. That is how our dependency on others increases, turning us into bystanders in our disaster response and therefore decreasing our resilience to deal with disaster. As a result, we won't improve after disasters and will be constantly off balance.

Disaster plans, for example, often read like boring instruction manuals, and disaster backpacks are never opened until the second they are needed. These tools can actually disempower you because they make you dependent on someone else to handle the disaster for you.

The night before I wrote this, I went to the US Geological Survey website, which tracks all seismic activity in the United States, and discovered that there were four earthquakes in California the day before. They weren't strong enough to do any damage, so no one considered them disasters. I am going to teach you how to metaphorically take an 8.0-magnitude earthquake and turn it into a 1.2-magnitude earthquake. I want you to take what seems to be a catastrophic disaster and turn it into a ride at Universal Studios.

Disasters don't have to be doom and gloom. The key is to challenge yourself to *design* the disasters you face. You can rewire your life in a way that will make you look at disasters differently forever. I've called this book *Design Any Disaster* because I want you to learn that while you can't change a given *incident*, you can prevent it from becoming a *disaster*.

Make no mistake—incidents are going to occur no matter what. But you can become 99.97 percent resilient against them. That may seem like a strange number to assign, but my approach to disasters is like the hand sanitizer in your pocket. It can't get every germ and bacterium, but it can get the vast majority of them. In the same way, I can't promise that the method I will show you in this book will completely eliminate disasters, because it can't. But it can get 99.97 percent of them.

Unless some magical technology is invented to prevent them, there will always be tornadoes, blizzards, earthquakes, and hurricanes. The history of humanity has proven that there will always be engineering failures no matter how advanced a structure is or how "unsinkable" a ship is, and, unfortunately, there will always be dangerous people and organizations who seek to harm innocent people.

That being said, just because danger is inevitable doesn't mean it has to destroy your life or control how you live it. I want you to look at disasters exactly as they are: a hurricane is just a windy rainstorm, an earthquake is just the ground shaking, and a bridge collapse is a metal structure failing. That is how you transform them into a ride at an amusement park. I'm not saying that you're going to forget what happens in these incidents—I still vividly remember the Universal Studios ride even after all these years, just as I have memories of every disaster I have experienced. However, their impact on how you live your life can either make you stronger for them or weaker. And whatever choice is made is totally up to you.

So how do you do that?

As I mentioned above, what causes a disaster to be more severe is not its size, the number of buildings destroyed, or the financial impact. It has nothing to do with any of those things. It's based on your *dependence* during the disaster. This dependence leaves you completely open to relying on someone else to conduct your disaster preparedness, response, and recovery. That is how you should judge the effect of a disaster: how much it disrupts your life to the point where you can't make yourself stronger afterward—otherwise known as *resilience*.

Over the next fifteen chapters, I'm going to teach you how to transform incidents into Universal Studio rides and how to safely keep yourself in the tram. The C3 Method is a simple yet revolutionary way to get you out of inaction and ready to deal with any kind of incident. I have used this method with thousands of clients all over the world—from corporations to nursing homes; to campgrounds, bars, and restaurants; to communities; to individual families of all kinds; to golf courses; to that little noodle shop on your neighborhood corner.

BREAKING DOWN THE C3 METHOD

What is the C3 Method? It's a framework that, for the first time, you can use in any phase of a given incident, from way before it strikes until you've fully recovered from it. The key is to take control of the disaster and lead yourself, your family, your business, and your life. Instead of simply becoming a bystander who does nothing, with the C3 Method you can take the steps to put yourself in a position where you can be an empowered leader among the people dealing with a disaster.

I want you to forget about everything you think you know about disasters. Not some things. Not a few things here and there. *Everything.* Everything you've read online, everything you've seen on television or in the movies, everything you've been told—because everything you have heard about disasters is 100 percent wrong. I want you to know that you don't have to be a victim in a disaster, *ever.*

I am going to challenge you throughout this book to make your life more resilient by decreasing the dependency on others that turns you into a disaster victim and by increasing your self-sufficiency. That's how you *Design Any Disaster.*

Disasters are only disasters in how they affect your life. If you can make your life more resilient, stronger, and better prepared in the way I outline in this book, *I can minimize 99.97 percent of any disaster you face just by decreasing your dependence.* You can do it. It just requires a systematic approach, which you'll gain through the C3 Method, a distillation of the tools I have used with people and organizations over a nearly twenty-year career. This method will fundamentally change how you view disaster plans, first-aid kits, red emergency backpacks, the doom-and-gloom mindset, government disaster services, donations, and every other element of disasters.

The three parts of the C3 Method are Command, Communicate, and Carry Out. *Command* will start by challenging your mindset regarding disasters. It will force you to change your default, dependent assumption that "if I do nothing, someone else will take care of it" to a mindset of "if I do nothing, no one else will." *Communicate* will take you on the affirmative step to creating a disaster team and assembling mechanisms to ensure a clear information exchange. Finally, in *Carry Out*, you will learn how to empower those around you in a disaster, providing clear, rational, and proven steps to give you the edge in any emergency. What you will discover is that these three planks, put together, open new doors in any disaster response.

By implementing the C3 Method, you will discover the critical secret I share in each of my disaster programs: *disasters are only disasters if you let them be*. Dangerous and unexpected incidents will occur regardless of what you do, but how you react to them and how they impact you make all the difference.

CHRONOLOGY OF A DISASTER

Most people think of disasters simply in terms of before, during, and after. But disaster response is a much more detailed continuum, with each phase feeding into the next. I have organized this book around what I believe to be a cycle that accurately reflects our ability to conquer disasters: Ready, React, Respond, Recover, Reverse.

Chapter one will introduce you to the C3 Method, covering each plank of the process and how to apply them in real incidents. Then you'll enter into part one of the book.

Part one is entitled "Ready: Prepare Yourself for Any Disaster with the C3 Method." Chapter two will begin with a discussion of the foundational documents of emergency preparedness: disaster plans. You will learn how disaster plans systematically disempower you through both their content as well as their format, and how the C3 Method can transform them into effective, dynamic documents. Chapter three will discuss Equipment, Supplies, and Technology (EST). You will learn that most EST make you *less* prepared and perpetuate negative behaviors that will weaken you throughout a disaster response by giving you a false sense of security, making you more dependent on outside agencies, organizations, or people. However, I will provide a framework for identifying and purchasing EST that will increase your preparedness for disasters. In chapter four, we'll discuss the useless emergency drills and training that seem to never accurately simulate real disasters. I'll teach you a simple trick I developed as a high-school drama student that will make these exercises infinitely better for you. It will outline how the C3 Method can transform these inane activities into effective and exciting disaster simulations.

Part two builds upon the opening chapters, discussing how to "Seize Control Seconds After Disaster Strikes with the C3 Method." Chapter five will address the panic response you feel the instant disaster strikes and how, instead of fighting that feeling, you can redirect that energy into an incredible tool by using a technique from a hundred-year-old martial art. Chapter six will round out the "React" phase of the disaster by providing you with tools that might save your life in a disaster. It will outline how to protect yourself from becoming a victim by applying a simple safety strategy.

Part three will help you "Conquer the 'Lights and Sirens' Phase Using the C3 Method" by giving you tools to respond to the immediate impacts of a disaster. Chapter seven will start off by identifying the three major responses to a disaster: evacuating, sheltering in place, and locking down. The chapter will teach you how to apply the C3 Method to each of these responses and identify best practices for any emergency. Chapter eight will take the next step, providing you with information on how to stabilize the disaster, including what you should take with you during an evacuation and what critical items you might forget. It will give you a new way to think about these items and about how to consider their implications for your ultimate disaster recovery. Part three will conclude in chapter nine by discussing what should be your last priority: property protection. Using the C3 Method, this chapter will give you a five-step process to evaluate any item in your home in just minutes.

Part four, "Recover: Restore Your Life in Five Sentences Using the C3 Method," will completely upend your thinking on how to recover after a disaster. With the C3 Method, you will discover a fast, easy-to-use methodology to approach any disaster with the "One Sentence Recovery." You will learn how to develop a custom disaster recovery for yourself using just one sentence that I will explore with you in part four's three chapters. Chapter ten will take you through the first part of the sentence to help you identify what needs to be recovered. Through a custom example, you will learn step-by-step how to determine the priorities of your recovery and the important difference between recovery and "going back to normal." Chapter eleven will take you through the second part of the sentence, helping you discern the time and cost of your recovery as you develop one that fits your budget and your timeline. Chapter twelve will bring you through the third and final part of the Recovery Sentence with an in-depth discussion of the strategies to employ when designing your recovery.

Continuing to break new ground, **part five** is a section that you will not find in any other disaster book. Here, in "Reverse: Transform Disaster into Opportunity with the C3 Method," you will discover the tools and strategies for turning any disaster into an opportunity to transform yourself, your community, and your future. I will share the secret I have discovered by working with thousands of organizations of how to completely change your mindset when dealing with a disaster. In chapter thirteen, you will discover the way to improve your life in the wake of a disaster. It will challenge you to refocus your attention away from what the disaster has destroyed and instead toward what it has revealed and how you can maximize this to your advantage. Chapter fourteen will extend this to the people around you and give you real tools to empower you to make real change during disasters that affect your community. Chapter fifteen will then round out the book by outlining how a lesson from an indigenous tribe in Indonesia can give you the key mindset to live in harmony with anything you face during the Age of Disasters.

CONCLUSION

What you will ultimately learn in these fifteen chapters is a cutting-edge, proven method for not just strengthening yourself but also learning the ability to design any disaster so that you can form your own elite disaster-response team for your life. These are strategies I have developed from working with thousands of clients around the world, from Fortune 500 companies to high-net-worth families, small businesses, schools of all types, and people just like you. I'm confident that you can define the disasters you will face for yourself, for your family, and for your community so that you can become stronger, safer, and more resilient after the disasters occur. You can conquer *any* disaster. You may have read other disaster books before this one, scrolled through disaster-recovery blog posts, or watched disaster movies. But if you think this book will be like those, then I think *Design Any Disaster* might just surprise you.

You will discover not basic techniques but a comprehensive, innovative approach that will transform how you prepare for, respond to, and recover from disasters. That is what *Design Any Disaster* is all about. Read on and let me show you how.

Chapter One

HOW THE C3 METHOD CAN DESIGN ANY DISASTER

O n a hot summer day in Southern California, when I was eighteen years old, my then-girlfriend and I decided to go to Disneyland. I had just graduated high school, was a newly minted EMT, and had just secured a job at a local ambulance company. We were in the ticketing area with a thousand tourists and lots of excited little kids, their parents waiting in long lines to buy their tickets and enter the park. Just as we walked up to get our tickets, however, something caught my eye, and I stared at the small crowd that had suddenly gathered nearby. People were standing in a half circle, milling around and looking nervous. There was a palpable sense that something unusual was going on, so I walked over to them.

I tried to figure out what was going on, but I couldn't quite see. After pushing my way through the crowd, I noticed a middle-aged man on the ground, unconscious. It looked like he had been clutching his chest. As I scanned the group, I saw that everyone was looking around nervously, some with their hands over their mouths, others sounding stressed in their quiet conversations.

Then it dawned on me. No one was going to do anything.

Like everyone else, I was shocked at the sight. However, I immediately said out loud, "What's going on here?" and got no response. So I shook the unconscious man to try to wake him up. When he didn't wake, I checked his pulse. There was none. I quickly realized that if I did nothing, no one else was going to do anything, either, so I pointed at someone and said, "You call 911."

I pointed at the next person and said, "You contact Disney staff."

Then I asked out loud, "Does anyone know CPR?" A woman in the back of the crowd stepped forward. I told her, "You and I are going to do CPR. You do the compressions, and I will do the rescue breaths."

Then I clapped my hands. The instant I did so, every single person did exactly as I had directed—without exception. The first person pulled out their cell phone and started calling 911. The second person ran a dead sprint to the first Disney employee they could find. And the woman and I started doing CPR together until professional rescuers arrived.

Let me ask you something. Why didn't those people start doing anything before I arrived? It was obviously an emergency, right? It didn't take a Harvard Medical School graduate to figure out that the man was in trouble. The hands clutching at his chest and his unconscious state were clear-cut signs.[16]

If we had not acted together as a team, that man probably would have died. He would have died because nobody would have done anything about it. And we would have just left him there. But once I empowered the people around me, we instantly turned into an elite team of responders.

That day at Disneyland, the crowd recognized that an emergency was occurring, but why was it that nobody in that group did anything about it? Were they just a group of psychopaths? Probably not, but this is a perfect microscopic example of what disasters are really like. This was a fairly common incident of a medical emergency, and what the crowd exemplified is a just a small sample of the way entire populations of people act during disasters. The group had two choices: do nothing or do something. It chose to do nothing—but why?

The answer is because nobody was empowered to act. Nobody was empowered to act because *everybody assumed that someone else was going to handle it.* Every single person assumed the exact same thing. Therefore, everybody was unempowered; everyone was like a victim—staying completely helpless and not doing anything.

This is a classic example of the Bystander Effect, a phenomenon in which people fail to offer needed help in emergencies. It occurs when the presence of others discourages an individual from intervening in an emergency situation.[17]

The phrase was originally coined after a famous incident in New York City when a woman named Kitty Genovese was murdered while dozens of neighbors who heard the attack did not alert authorities. While the original story is under question by historians, the concept stuck and has been attributed to several other famous incidents.[18]

This is a phenomenon I see all the time in disaster management because so many people are bystanders in their own disaster responses. Yes, they notice something is going on and know it's a disaster, but they don't want to take responsibility for it because they feel as though someone else will handle it for them. This increase in your dependency on others turns you into a bystander, disempowering you and decreasing your resilience.

As you will discover, the Bystander Effect shows up in every aspect of disasters. People make this mistake when writing or reviewing useless disaster plans, purchasing unnecessary disaster equipment, or running boring disaster drills. When you assume that someone else will largely handle an emergency, you leave your evacuation decisions to government agencies and expect well-meaning nonprofits to save you and your family. When you do that, you increase your dependence, which then turns you into a bystander and sends your resilience plummeting.

DISASTER PREPAREDNESS, RESPONSE, AND RECOVERY DISEMPOWER YOU

Disaster readiness, response, and recovery can completely disempower you. The reason isn't the disaster itself. You can be disempowered because you may assume that if you do nothing, someone else will do it for you. When you do this, you are essentially allowing someone else to design the disaster for you. And when you surrender control of the disaster, you basically place yourself in the hands of someone else. *This is what turns you into a bystander.*

This happens when you aren't in an assertive mindset—only a reactive one. This is important because when you're in a reactive mode, you can't Communicate effectively, form your own team, or empower anyone else. Disasters can't be handled alone. From evacuation to recovery, there are going to be many tasks to complete. If you and those around you remain passive, you won't be able to effectively Carry Out the steps necessary before, during, or after a disaster. These steps aren't always complex, but they must all be completed. Without an assertive mindset to empower yourself and others, you'll get a poor incident response.

YOU DON'T HAVE A CONSISTENT FRAMEWORK FOR DISASTERS

This can all be rectified if we apply a consistent framework to disasters. But most of us don't, and as a result, we respond to disasters in an unpredictable manner. Without predictability, you increase your dependency on someone else because, lacking empowerment, you easily become a bystander. And that "someone else" is usually government emergency managers. When you respond to a disaster without any kind of consistent framework, you are basically handing control of it to forces totally outside of your control.

If you depend on the government to handle an emergency for you, then I can guarantee it's going to be a disaster. Most county emergency-management agencies have two or three employees, of which one will likely be an administrative employee (not a disaster preparedness professional). That means a very small and potentially underequipped team will be in charge of an entire county by itself.

The goal of an effective disaster strategy is to minimize your dependency on others and to hand you effective control over how a disaster will impact your life. It should give you a series of predicable, repeatable steps to help you become more self-reliant. The longer it takes to get there, however, the more dependent you become. This is why people do not do well during a disaster; disasters significantly worsen the longer you wait to respond effectively to them. Many people think that disasters run on a singular chronological line when, in fact, the process is a circle. The five points on this circle, which correspond to the five parts of this book, represent the life cycle of any disaster: Ready, React, Respond, Recover, and Reverse. And each point of the circle is fiercely dependent on the previous one. So when one phase begins to fail, a cascading series of failures will then occur.

Diagram 1.1

Ready: This is where disaster preparedness occurs, including writing disaster plans, buying equipment, training, running drills, and engaging in what we call "mitigation activities," such as putting up sandbags prior to a flood, boarding windows ahead of a hurricane, or cutting dead trees prior to the wildfire season.

React: This is the immediate phase after disaster strikes. It starts with what I term the "gasp," the moment when we realize a disaster is occurring. This phase also involves how we handle the immediate stages following a disaster.

Respond: This is what I call the "lights-and-sirens" phase of disasters. It's the part of disasters we see the most on television: people evacuating out of a burning building, cars sitting on the freeway in evacuation traffic jams, hundreds of people laying on cots in school gymnasiums, general mayhem as people are being carried off in floodwater. There are firefighters and the military and lots of people in uniform. There are reporters everywhere covering stories about rescues and people in shelters.

Recover: This is where we try to restore our basic life functions after the disruption of a disaster. While many would say this is synonymous with getting things "back to normal," I'd argue that this idea is completely incorrect. During the recovery from a disaster, you identify the critical elements of your life that have been disrupted in the emergency and get them functioning again. When you "get back to normal," the goal is to try to reconstruct and restore your life to exactly the way it was before: every television, every window, every piece of furniture.

Reverse: This is the final phase of a disaster. In this pioneering step, I want to entirely change your thinking—I want you to turn the disaster into something that makes you stronger and better. I will show you how to coexist with incidents and how to position your life so that you can *eliminate* the disaster, no matter how large the incident.

The impact of not being fully prepared in all five stages of disaster response is that your response can suddenly devolve into exactly what we see on television: confusion, chaos, and panic. This then increases your dependence and the Bystander Effect. The fact, again, is this: as you increase your dependency on others throughout this cycle, you decrease your disaster resilience and become more of a bystander.

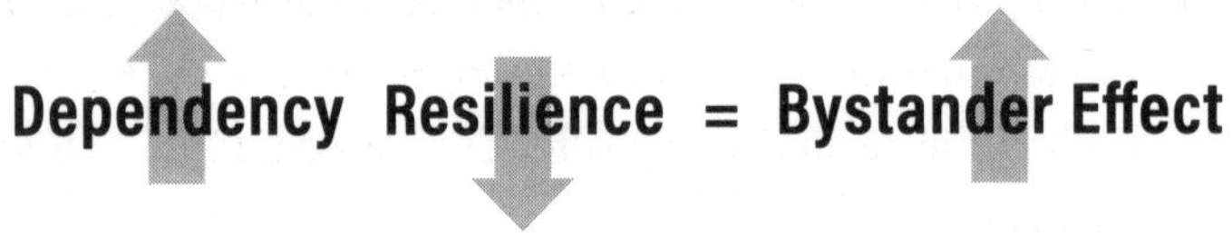

Dependency Resilience = Bystander Effect

Diagram 1.2

Your preparedness is not based on the number of pages in your disaster plan or how many flashlights you have or how many days of food you have stored in your home. It's based on how dependent you are on other people in your response to an incident. Instead of looking at how many pages are in the plan that you have or how many square feet of defensible space you've created in your house, ask yourself: How dependent am I on someone or something else to respond to emergencies for me?

Who are you most dependent on during a disaster? If it's not you, you're in trouble.

And if it's not you, then someone or something else is designing your disaster—whether a certain piece of an equipment, a particular agency, or chance itself. Companies large and small, organizations, and families in all societies make this same mistake with terrible consequences, but there is a way to avoid it.

C3 METHOD SOLUTIONS

Traditional disaster books will tell you what to buy and micromanage your disaster response. I'm not going to do that. If you want to know the first three things you must do in an earthquake, you bought the wrong disaster book (okay, if you insist: drop, cover, and hold on). I am going to go beyond that . . . much further beyond. I want to focus your thinking so that when you have to make important response decisions, you have the right approach to make them most effectively. I don't want you to fall into the Bystander Effect when dealing with disasters where you live because if you do, you won't just be less prepared to handle the situation—you'll permanently lose control of it.

So I am going to introduce you to the C3 Method. This method is one I developed working with small businesses and families around the world. It's powerful because it can be applied to all five points of the disaster cycle and gives you momentum to move to the next one. The three parts of the C3 Method are Command, Communicate, and Carry Out. Each is critical to reassert control over a given incident.

COMMAND   COMMUNICATE   CARRY-OUT

Diagram 1.3

As you progress through each one, you will discover that they build upon one another by doing two things: decreasing your dependency on someone else and increasing your independence.

COMMAND - "I CAN EMPOWER MYSELF"

The first step in the C3 Method is Command. What does that mean? While I know "Command" sounds very military, I don't mean it completely in the military sense, with ranks and orders. What I really mean by Command is taking leadership over a disaster. Command is purely a mindset. When you take Command, you are hijacking your mindset from the poisonous passivity of the Bystander Effect that says, "If I do nothing, someone else will handle it" to a powerful mindset of "If I do nothing, no one else will, either." This is a critical difference. Disaster after disaster has demonstrated that those who assert this active, self-empowered mindset are the ones who conquer any threat.

Therefore, I want to challenge you to recalibrate your thinking in a disaster: instead of assuming that someone else will handle it, in *EVERY* disaster, *EVERY* incident, *EVERY* emergency, no matter how big or small, *I want you to assume that if you do nothing, no one else will, either.* If you only do one thing going forward, let it be to make every decision in a disaster based on this assumption alone—because this allows you to empower yourself.

So whether you are approaching the writing of a disaster plan, buying equipment, evacuating a flood, or recovering your life after a disaster, the first step is always taking Command by fundamentally changing your thinking. Most people don't do this, which is why people make the same mistakes in countless disasters.

In my Disneyland example, the Bystander Effect was on full display in front of everyone because no one wanted to intervene—because everyone assumed the same thing: that someone else would handle it. Everyone was instantly turned into a bystander in the emergency because *everyone assumed that someone else was going to handle it.* Therefore, everyone remained frozen in inaction, letting the disaster control them instead of taking control over their response to the disaster. This in turn effectively made them victims. This happens in disaster after disaster. Someone will house me; someone will feed me; someone will give me money. Others can certainly provide help, but you should never assume that they will because this increases your dependency on them, increases your bystanderism, and therefore decreases your disaster preparedness.

I want to reemphasize this for you in the strongest possible terms: every time you see a disaster, instead of assuming someone else will handle it—in *every disaster, every incident, every emergency*, no matter its scale, whether it's a natural disaster, a technological disaster, a security disaster, or a common disaster—I want you to assume that you must act, or no one else will. I don't care if you have a big family or if you're working for a business or nonprofit with many people who could step up; I want you to assume that none of them will act. Assume that everyone else is lazy and won't do a thing. Assume that you are the only one who can help and that your leadership will make the difference. Take Command from the beginning to jump-start the C3 Method.

You'll quickly notice the difference when Command is taken on a scene. Let's pretend you were at Disneyland with me. Suddenly, you see a man who is unconscious on the ground. If you tell yourself that someone else will handle it, you will just watch or walk away, frozen in a state of inaction. Now, change your assumption: if you don't do anything, no one is going to help him, which means he will likely die. See how a small change in mindset will completely alter your approach to an emergency? That's the essence of taking Command.

Taking Command in a disaster can take many forms. It could be taking charge during a medical emergency or overseeing your family's evacuation after a nuclear emergency at a local plant. The key is to use an empowering mindset to gain agency over the disaster. That doesn't mean you have to be the sole leader in charge—you can also Command by delegating roles left and right to others. By Commanding, you can conquer any emergency or disaster you face, no matter how large. And with the tools I'll give you, you'll never feel overwhelmed again because you'll be empowered to lead and work with your team. The ultimate purpose of taking Command is to counter the Bystander Effect, which is something I see in every phase of a disaster.

The C3 Method is so powerful that you can be in Command even if you are a member of a vulnerable population because you'll know how to empower yourself and those around you. I have worked with vulnerable populations and taught this exact concept to them when giving them disaster-plan advice and tools to help them retain complete control over their own disaster responses.

At Disneyland, I took Command of the emergency right away—you can see the C3 Method in practice. But you might be wondering: Why in the world did any of the people in the crowd listen to me? I wasn't the CEO of Disney (although that seems like a great job). I wasn't wearing a uniform, and I was probably the youngest person in that crowd. But I took responsibility for the emergency, and even though I didn't know the man on the ground, I decided to take full accountability for his care. The emergency became *my* emergency. This was all part of taking Command—and by doing so, I was able to empower myself and the people around me to jump into action.

This can apply at your work, home, or school. Take Command no matter what, and you'll see what a big difference it makes in an emergency. While taking Command doesn't mean you are going to be in charge of everything, it does create a process for assigning individual responsibility. You can follow instructions and still absolutely be in Command. For instance, let's say you're a student at a school. Taking Command doesn't mean you are going to run the school when a disaster occurs. What it does mean is that when disaster strikes, you will maximize your potential by empowering those around you, whether your fellow students or the teacher, to act by grabbing equipment, getting people out, and following instructions. Taking Command means choosing not to be a passive bystander.

If something happens to your teacher—or let's say they become injured or incapacitated—you can take Command by grabbing the class roster, making sure you have the emergency backpack before you leave the classroom, and initiating an evacuation if it's appropriate to the situation.

People in business tell me all the time that their manager will handle things in an emergency. Let's say you work at a tech company, and the manager is hit in the head when an object falls from the ceiling during an earthquake. Suddenly, your leader is gone. So you pick up the plan and start the disaster procedures yourself. That sounds a lot better than waiting for another manager to come handle it for you, right?

One afternoon, I was driving to a presentation in Phoenix, Arizona. Just north of the city, I noticed a mattress in my lane on the freeway. I had no idea how long it had been there, but I quickly jerked the wheel to evade it and then continued down the freeway until I could pull over to call 911. Once the call connected, the dispatcher asked what the nature of the emergency was. I informed her of the mattress and its approximate location. While she was typing, I said, "I'm sure you've gotten a dozen calls on this already."

You know what she told me? Not only was there no avalanche of calls—I was the first one to call about it at all.

Dozens of cars must have passed that mattress. Not a single person was willing or able to take Command—in this case, taking responsibility for it and calling 911 to prevent potential accidents on the road. I'm confident everyone assumed that somebody else was going to handle it.

While the mattress in Arizona was a relatively minor incident (though it wouldn't have been so minor if it had caused an accident), it also highlights the importance of shifting one's mindset and taking Command. I had to be the one to take charge over the situation. If other motorists had decided to take Command as well, that would've been even better. The point is that we must take responsibility to address the emergencies we encounter and seek help from those who can act on the situation, and we must not quit until the issues are resolved.

First responders take Command by selecting a person to assume the Incident Commander (IC) role. The IC is the person on scene who is ultimately responsible for ensuring that the response is carried out effectively and safely.[19] There is an IC appointed in any disaster, whether large or small. Even during Hurricane Harvey and the BP oil spill in 2010, there was a single IC who ran each operation.[20]

An IC doesn't have to do everything, though. In fact, as you will discover, delegation is one of an IC's strongest tools. But ultimately, the effective and efficient execution of tasks is the final responsibility of the IC. That is what I want you to do as well. You can be the IC in any disaster or emergency. I have written disaster plans for families of all kinds (including those of vulnerable populations), restaurants, bars, nursing homes, RV parks, apiaries, alligator farms, and many others. For every one of those groups, without exception, I instructed them on how to appoint an IC and ensure that they have someone ultimately accountable during an emergency.

The problem I often see regarding Command within families, businesses, and organizations of all sizes is that no one wants to be the one to make a final decision in a disaster. This leads to the feeling of needing to endlessly collaborate. You must stop this. This is not disaster response by committee. One person has to be ultimately accountable. That doesn't mean, however, that you shouldn't take anyone else's advice or counsel into consideration. In fact, I believe the advice of others is so critical that I have built it in directly as the second step to the C3 Method: Communicate.

COMMUNICATE - "I CAN EMPOWER OTHERS"

Now that you have taken Command, you must Communicate. Communication might seem like a simple concept if I asked you for the dictionary definition. You'd do a quick search and say something like, "It's the act or process of communicating; the imparting or interchange of thoughts, opinions, or information by speech, writing, or signs."

We all have a kind of working definition for communication: relaying information from one person to another, whether it is written, verbal, or non-verbal. But in a disaster, communication is more than just giving assignments to people. There is a bigger use for it. I want to change your definition of communication. Here's how I want you to define it instead: it's the act of *organizing and leading a team* during an emergency. I want you to assemble a team that works together when you face a disaster, like I did at Disneyland.

It doesn't even matter if the members of your team know that they are on the team or not. For example, during a hurricane, the National Hurricane Center staff can be members of your team. That doesn't mean you have to pick up the phone and speak to the director. But you can pull up the website and gather the storm information you'll need to most effectively make decisions. By setting up a communication pipeline between yourself and the people who can help you, you then become a team. This process can be unidirectional or bidirectional.

This was the team I formed at Disneyland:

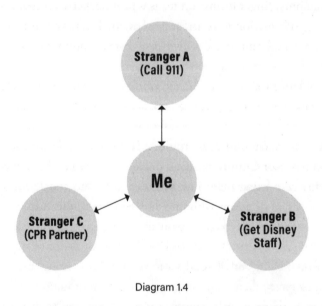

Diagram 1.4

Your team should include people who can help you directly, like family and friends. I call these "direct team members" because you have direct contact with them and therefore can establish a bidirectional communication pipeline.

But your team should also include those who can advise you, like news sources, government and first-response agencies, doctors, colleagues, and even your workplace. I call these "indirect team members" because you can only listen to what they tell you and cannot generally speak to them, creating a unidirectional communication pathway.

When you Communicate effectively, you'll stop relying on others and assuming that someone else will handle the disaster because you'll be designing and assembling your own team of people without having to wait for someone to do it for you. This combats the Bystander Effect by decreasing your dependence, since you'll be the one personally selecting people and organizations to help you.

Communication is without a doubt the weakest part of most disaster responses. The common image of disaster-response Communication put forward by movies and TV is one person yelling and barking orders at other people in a dictatorial fashion while everyone just blindly obeys. That's not it.

Communication means establishing a clear pipeline between yourself and those you are providing information to, as well as between yourself and the people providing information to you. That's what good teams do. It may seem simple, but you would be amazed at how many people Communicate ineffectively. I once worked a shift in a state emergency operations center (where government agencies meet during a disaster to determine where resources should be placed). I was on the overnight shift during a major flood activation. Around midnight, I was startled to hear two senior-level officials yelling at one another about using school buses as evacuation transportation. This was completely unempowering because that style of Communication only treats people like ineffectual lemmings instead of putting them in a position to be successful. You can't make clear, well-reasoned decisions without effective Communication.

Disasters will be very busy, with many things happening simultaneously, and it is very easy for the Command established in the first step of the C3 Method to be quickly lost if solid Communication is not demonstrated and maintained properly.

The two steps work in tandem as well. Commanding will significantly enhance your ability to Communicate effectively, which will then decrease your dependence, because it gives you the ability to gather the information you need to be effective. Once you have clarity around what needs to be done, your

Communication will become much more effective—whether that's gathering disaster plans, equipment, and supplies or determining the location of hazards within a community during an evacuation after a major natural disaster. And without an effective team, your response won't be effective because, frankly, disasters can't be handled alone.

Communication will in turn significantly enhance your ability to Command because it gives you the information you need and the information you must provide to others. In first-response work, we use Communication to empower our colleagues to perform distinct tasks within an emergency. In a car accident, for example, the firefighters will work to extract victims from shattered cars and put out fires resulting from damaged engines, while police officers will block traffic, provide support to medical responders, and evaluate if drugs or alcohol were involved, and emergency medical services (EMS) personnel will treat victims and put them in ambulances for rapid transport to a local hospital. Each one of us, through Communication with each other, will provide the necessary information for everyone to be more empowered as a team on scene and more effective in Carrying Out their roles, which is the last of the three steps in the C3 Method.

CARRY OUT - "WE CAN EMPOWER EACH OTHER"

This one is easy: just do it. Get it done, whether that means going to the restaurant to get your own food or completing a complex rescue during a flood. In an emergency, it is important that you get things moving as soon as possible. Momentum is crucial throughout any disaster.

Once you have empowered your mindset and your team, every action you take needs to reinforce that empowerment. This means giving people manageable, simple tasks that utilize their strengths. At Disneyland, we were a team, and we completed tasks together as a team. I didn't try to do everything myself—that would have been impossible. I couldn't call 911, perform CPR, and grab Disney staff at the same time. But once I had empowered my team, we were able to empower each other by Communicating and getting tasks done toward a common goal. So all tasks that get Carried Out should be done so on this basis alone. You should complete actions as a team, together. As a result, you will no longer rely on others or assume that someone else will handle it.

You'll empower those around you to get tasks completed and can then design the disaster the way you want it to happen.

In a disaster, most people think they must try to do it all themselves. That's not how Carrying Out works. You should work as a team while still maintaining responsibility for the disaster. Carrying Out means that I am going to remain accountable for the tasks that must get completed and will make sure they are done. If a task isn't done, it will become my responsibility to complete it. With this mindset, when you encounter limitations, you won't make assumptions about whether a task has been completed because you'll know that you'll be eventually responsible for completing it yourself. It's crucial to recognize that if you don't assign or complete a task, no one else will, either. The key is to get things done by creating discrete tasks for which you will remain accountable. This will guarantee that you'll care and that you'll maintain an active mindset because the situation will become *your* disaster. Lead people by example, collaboration, and proper planning, and they, too, will be empowered to care.

It was a crisp Friday morning when an employee at a skilled nursing facility in South Carolina (a client facility of mine) smelled smoke. Since this is an unusual smell for a healthcare facility, she followed her nose to quickly trace the source. After exploring a couple of hallways, she opened the door to a community room where activities were held for residents of the nursing home, such as birthdays, bingo nights, and sing-alongs. What she encountered shocked her: the contents of a trash can had caught on fire, which had then ignited a nearby table. She noticed that all the combustible decorations had been left out after the celebration of a centenary birthday for one of the well-known residents at the facility.

Realizing the potential for a quick spread of the fire, she immediately secured the room by blocking it off. She then called out into the hallway to a nursing assistant who was administering medication nearby and told her to immediately go to the nurses' station and make an announcement for a supervisor and to be on standby to call 911. A second employee who arrived was told to get a fire extinguisher and to help move flammable objects out of the way. A third employee, hearing the commotion, then arrived, and my client told him to put all the residents who were in the hallway away from the room so that they would not smell the smoke and would be ready if evacuation became necessary. She then grabbed another fire extinguisher and began fire-suppression efforts.

In short order, the fire was finally put out, and they took stock of the damage to the room. The administrator, relieved that no one was hurt and that the fire had been contained to just a few easily replaceable items, decided to have a meeting to determine how the response went and how they could prevent such a thing from happening again. In the meeting, the administrator asked who the employee was who had taken the first steps to getting the fire under control. A hand in the back of the room was raised, and the administrator was struck dumb. The person who raised their hand had only been employed at the facility for a couple of weeks, and had only just taken my training days before.

At Disneyland, after getting things started, I made sure that everyone had their tasks and that I was supervising them to the end. If the person I had tasked with doing CPR with me hadn't done a good job with the compressions, I would have switched with her to give rescue breaths. Or, if I had started to get tired, I would have asked for others in the crowd to help with the CPR. Either way, I was still responsible for Commanding the scene, Communicating the expectations, and seeing the tasks completed effectively.

Really solid Command and Communication makes Carrying Out tasks much more effective. They provide the foundation for seeing that tasks are completed well by empowering people when things are chaotic. A medical emergency with a single victim is one thing. A 7.5-magnitude earthquake with thousands of victims spread over dozens of square miles is something else—a complex situation that requires a sophisticated, organized response. But regardless of scope, any response strategy you employ that doesn't reinforce mechanisms of taking leadership of a scene, communicating tasks effectively, and ensuring they are effectively completed is doomed to fail.

The C3 Method is the most effective way of dealing with a disaster because it focuses your responsibility and ensures that you remain in total control of the incident.

When you apply the C3 Method correctly, you will never face the Bystander Effect again in any disaster situation. Let's say your community is struck by a major flash flood, which is fairly common in many areas. You notice that something is going on (a rush of dangerous water) and you interpret it as being an emergency (a danger to people and property), but then there comes the matter of responsibility. You may feel as though someone else is responsible for handling the flash flood and its effects. In part, you are right. The fire department and trained emergency crews will deal with the flood itself. But the flood's effects on your life are totally within your own control (Command). Once you have established that, you must get your family and/or colleagues organized (Communicate) and then implement the actions you need to take (Carry Out). By effectively executing these steps of the C3 Method, you will never find yourself in a situation where events are controlling you.

The C3 Method can be used in any incident—from inflation to insect invasions to even wedding disasters (like when the caterer doesn't show up)—at any time, as it puts you in control, establishes a plan for Communication, and gives you tools to ensure that tasks get completed quickly and efficiently. You will discover in the following chapters how to apply the C3 Method to each disaster-response stage: Ready, React, Respond, Recover, and Reverse.

CONCLUSION

The C3 Method is a simple yet powerful system to manage any incident and prevent it from becoming a worsening disaster. While you can't control the incident itself, you can control 99.97 percent of the impact it has on your life. Taking Command, Communicating, and Carrying Out will empower you in almost any incident you face.

In Disneyland, once staff and emergency services arrived at the scene, my three-person team was able to seamlessly hand off the man to them. I took the time to exchange handshakes and greetings with my impromptu disaster-response team and then watched the ambulance pull away. Sometimes people ask me what happened to the man. I don't know. But I do remember the team I assembled and how we were able, in a small way, to design the disaster.

Part One

READY

Prepare Yourself for Any
Disaster with the C3 Method

Chapter Two

DISASTER PLANS THAT ACTUALLY PREPARE YOU

On Saturday, January 13, 2018, at 8:07 AM local time, residents of and visitors to the Hawaiian Islands were greeted with this all-caps text message sent to their phones: "BALLISTIC MISSILE THREAT INBOUND TO HAWAII. SEEK IMMEDIATE SHELTER. THIS IS NOT A DRILL." This alert led people to believe that North Korea or another belligerent nuclear state had launched a first-strike missile on the United States with Hawaii as the target. As you can imagine, there was widespread panic and confusion. People called loved ones for final goodbyes and prepared for the inevitable detonation that would wipe most of humanity from the Hawaiian Islands.

One of those individuals visiting the island was a client of mine, who immediately after reading the text message sprinted to the front desk of the four-star hotel where she was staying to determine where she should go to shelter in place. The scene that confronted her in the lobby could only be described as total pandemonium. Guests ran around yelling hysterically at employees, trying to figure out what to do. The front-desk clerks were completely overwhelmed and desperately tried to regain control of the situation. Somehow threading through the crowd, my client approached the front desk in a vain attempt to get information. No one responded to her, as the employees were occupied with trying, without success, to reach the manager on the radio, who was across the property dealing with an unrelated guest matter and hadn't yet seen the text message.

Behind the front desk, staff members leafed through the property's disaster plan: a thick, disorganized red binder with lots of random Post-it notes and loose-leaf paper. In the confusion, my client managed a quick glance at the plan and was able to make out the instructions in case of an emergency: "Call the manager and wait for instructions."

Most disaster plans I have read are terrible. Not only are they often completely ineffective at providing the authority, policies, and procedures necessary to respond to a disaster, but they are also poorly maintained. However, the main reason why so many disaster plans are completely ineffective is because, either explicitly or implicitly, they deliver the same message in that Hawaiian hotel disaster plan: *someone else will handle the disaster for you*. Someone else will take *Command* and lead, someone else will *Communicate* and organize a team, and someone else will *Carry Out* the tasks.

This means that disaster plans can actually make you less prepared because they encourage you to be wholly dependent on someone else, turning you into a helpless bystander. They seem to be designed to put people in positions where they'll be ineffective. The question I ask when I read plans like this is: Why have a plan at all?

The sad irony here is that having a terrible disaster plan defeats the purpose of having a disaster plan in the first place. It immediately disempowers you from doing anything. This is a shame because a competently written disaster plan is an incredibly valuable tool in saving lives and protecting property. To be effective, however, disaster plans must do more than just tell you where the can opener or fire extinguisher is located; they must empower you to be able to complete tasks effectively. If they don't do this, the procedures outlined in a disaster plan become useless.

Before I go over the details of this, I think it will be helpful to start with the basic anatomy of a good disaster plan for an individual or family. Such disaster plans ultimately consist of three sub-plans:

- The crisis preparedness plan
- The emergency response plan
- The disaster recovery plan

Each of these plans is associated with a separate time in the cycle of a disaster. As is indicated in the name, the disaster-preparedness plan deals with the Ready phase of disasters: disaster planning, equipment gathering, training, and drills. An emergency-response plan focuses on the React and Respond phases of a disaster, mostly dealing with health, safety, and stabilizing the incident. Finally, the disaster-recovery plan deals with the Recovery phase of an emergency. In the disaster-recovery plans I write, I also include my cutting-edge Reverse phase because I want my clients to be stronger than they were before the disaster.

YOU DON'T WRITE PLANS FOR YOURSELF

It's astonishing to me how many people don't have a plan at all, as it's a powerful tool for managing a disaster. I think part of the reason is that most people think they don't need a plan. They feel that they can navigate a disaster based upon previous experience. However, this is a serious mistake because when you don't plan, that doesn't mean you don't have one. It just means that someone else is planning for you.

If you live in one of the approximately 3,100 counties in the United States, there is, without exception, an emergency operations plan that details how residents of your county should respond to a disaster. It lays out the roads and evacuation routes, as well as plans for sheltering and feeding the population and ensuring continuity of the water supply. This all sounds good until you realize that you will have to follow this plan's steps *simultaneously* with *every other person in your county*.

If you do not have a plan, this county-made plan is now your plan.

Without a plan of your own, you are assuming that if you do nothing, your county will handle it for you. You will have no control over the plan or its provisions because you did not create it; government bureaucrats did. It may still seem tempting to just go along with the county-made emergency plan, but doing so actually increases your dependence.

By not writing a disaster plan, you have decided that other organizations will do everything for you. This decreases your preparedness because you will have relinquished control. Other people will run your evacuation, your sheltering, and your professional future. Do you want them to run your life after a disaster?

YOU CAN'T ACCESS CRITICAL DISASTER PLANS THAT WILL AFFECT YOU

What I often see is that people can't or don't access the disaster plans that will directly impact their lives. This manifests in several ways, depending on the organizations involved, but the ultimate result is this: it is *way* too difficult to get ahold of the plan.

In the private sector (particularly in large companies), I see disaster plans that cover the usual parade of horrors: storms, earthquakes, terrorism, etc. Often, these are plans printed on colorful laminated paper and hung on the wall that lay out what to do in the first sixty seconds of a disaster. But a plan on a wall isn't enough. It can cover some preliminary steps, but it won't come close to covering everything you must know in a disaster response because disasters can last days, weeks, or even months.

The longer version of a disaster plan, however, is almost always unavailable. When someone wants to read a full version, they are often confronted by security and asked why they want the plan. Alternatively, especially in the hospitality industry or other locally managed properties, organizations will keep a copy of the full plan squirreled away in a manager's office. I have spoken to employees who have told me that they didn't want to ask for a copy because they didn't want to draw attention to themselves. There is absolutely no reason that an emergency-response plan should be kept from a workforce.

In many cases, even if the basic emergency-response plan is available, business continuity plans (BCPs), crisis communication plans, and risk assessments are never made available. It's a complete mystery to me as to why this is the case. If the company you are working for has a major disaster, the BCP will tell you when the company should begin its recovery and when it must have its critical processes and operations functioning. In other words, it should tell you when they plan to reopen for business. It also provides a roadmap as to how this will happen. At the start of the COVID-19 pandemic, one of the biggest uncertainties of employees working for companies large and small was when and how they would be able to return to work. A competently written BCP provides this kind of information in clear text and is therefore a critical tool for you that should be made available.

You deserve to know the ultimate impact a disaster will have on your long-term future at a company. Throughout the COVID-19 pandemic, workers have discovered the hard way that there may be unadvertised policies and procedures regarding payment when working remotely. Salaries have also been impacted, particularly when adjusted against the cost of living in a particular geographic area.

When you are not provided this information, you lack some of the necessary information to prepare adequately for a disaster. What if a company you rely upon as your single source of income to feed and house your family is impacted by a flood, and its disaster plan explains that it doesn't plan to recover at all? Or what if they have no provisions for dealing with paychecks? Or what if the plan is to close the office after a disaster and turn everyone into a remote employee? You can easily become a bystander when you have no choice but to be dependent on a plan you can't even access. This decreases your resiliency and magnifies the effects of any disasters that occur.

THE PLANS ARE UNREADABLE

The biggest problem I see with disaster plans is that most are almost completely unreadable. I don't understand how companies can write disaster plans for employees with technical, legalistic ten-dollar words, put them into long paragraphs at ten-point font, and expect a regular person to read them. Ready for a snooze fest? Pick up your county's emergency operations plan: eight hundred pages of boring text with lots of technical nonsense and legal jargon—not exactly compelling narratives here. With these plans, finding the right steps and performing them in the right order requires a master's degree in emergency management.

In addition, plans that are supposed to be used in a disaster often include things like an authorization page, legal disclaimers, and a list of sources consulted by the writers. If you're in the midst of a disaster and need to use the plan, who cares who wrote it? Who cares what laws the plan relies upon? Nobody. That language slows people down and makes it hard for the average person to read through it efficiently. Therefore, the plan becomes inaccessible. But this is just the beginning. Let's look more closely at some of the common ways disaster plans are unreadable or miss the mark.

PLANS THAT ARE TOO LIMITED

Plans that cover disasters people are unlikely to face can be severely limited in their effectiveness. I once had a school on the Central Coast of California hire me to write its disaster plan. Like usual, I did my homework and reviewed what the ten most likely threats were to the school based upon FEMA flood maps, county assessments, photos of the property, and insurance assessment reports. However, as is my habit, I asked the client what they thought, based upon local knowledge, was their most likely disaster threat.

When I asked the principal, she told me with a straight face that she thought the biggest threat to her school was a terrorist attack that would result in her being beheaded live on the internet. She then instructed me to write the plan with this in mind. I counseled her about how misguided the plan would be as a result, but she was adamant. What resulted was a plan that did not accurately reflect the realities of the school and was focused so narrowly as to render much of the plan useless. By limiting the scope of a plan, its focus will shift to a narrow problem set.

PLANS THAT ARE OUT OF DATE

Obsolete disaster plans or ones with out-of-date information are very common but completely useless during an emergency. I remember my very first day on my very first job as an emergency manager. I was excited and nervous, waiting in my office for my boss to arrive. When she did, she had in her hands this really thick binder. She slammed the binder on my desk with a resounding thud and said to me, "This disaster plan was written by the best disaster planners in the world. These are people with, collectively, hundreds of years of experience. They spent years working on this plan. It's absolutely perfect." Then she paused and continued, "Which is why I want you to find one thing wrong with it. Good luck." Then she left. I guess that was one way to get a career started. Once she closed the door, I looked at the plan. I tried to figure out what I was going to do, and the binder just stared back.

I was completely overwhelmed as I scanned the pages for anything that I could improve upon. Page after page, I found nothing. Finally, I noticed a tab that read, "Emergency Contacts Page." I looked through it and found a list of names with associated phone numbers, so I started making phone calls. When I got to the fourth or fifth name and dialed the number, a woman answered.

I asked to speak to the person on the list, and after a silent pause, she told me calmly that I couldn't speak to him. The reason? He had been dead for the past five years. That was a serious problem because, in the disaster plan, he was responsible for coordinating federal and state disaster responses. If disaster were to strike, the response would be delayed for hours, maybe even days, trying to find a replacement. A plan written by people with hundreds of years of experience was rendered ineffective because of a bad phone number.

PLANS THAT SAY "DON'T TOUCH"

While unreadable, limited, and out-of-date plans are common, the vast majority of disaster plans self-destruct in the same way: people are told not to use them, much like the one at the Hawaiian hotel. There is nothing worse than a plan that does this. That is a guaranteed way to make sure your disaster response completely crashes and burns—because once you have disempowered everyone, then no one cares about having a plan in the first place. This is the reason I think so few businesses get a disaster plan in the first place, and the plans that do get created aren't worth the red binders that surround them.

The organizations that do make disaster plans stick them on a back shelf, never to be seen again. This problem is so prevalent that when my employees visit our clients for the first time, I tell them to run our famous "dust test." I developed this humorous, slightly unscientific test after looking at hundreds of neglected and forgotten disaster plans. During the "dust test," an employee runs their finger along the top of a disaster binder and determines the amount of dust that has accumulated. For every half-centimeter of dust on the finger, the plan is 25 percent less effective. I have discovered that the amount of dust is inversely proportional to how well a plan empowers the people expected to use it.

I was once hired by a healthcare company operating in the Carolinas that owned about a half-dozen nursing homes and was looking to totally revamp its disaster programs. I noticed that facility after facility contained employees who knew next to nothing about the old disaster plans. So one day, I decided to test out how far this went on an unsuspecting nurse. I approached one of the nurses' stations, identified myself, and asked to see a copy of the disaster plan. The plan should have been easy to find, as plans should be ready for use as soon as disaster strikes. Little did she realize that I had actually already found the disaster plan. It was in a red binder on an eye-level shelf behind her head.

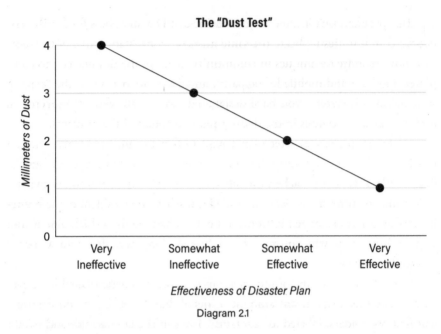

The "Dust Test"

Effectiveness of Disaster Plan

Diagram 2.1

But, feigning ignorance, I asked her to find it for me. She said she would look for it. I came back about an hour later and asked her if she had been able to find it. She told me she had looked for it and asked around, but no one knew where it was. The disaster plan was still sitting directly behind her head.

In business, the most common way this manifests is when a company's disaster plan expressly instructs employees to seek authorization from a manager before doing anything in the plan. It's as if the plan writers specifically don't trust the employees to respond to an emergency, and so they don't take the risk of giving them any responsibility whatsoever. This really annoys me because what the guests in the lobby of that Hawaiian hotel experienced is always the result of this idiotic policy: in an instant, employees become bystanders with little direct role in the disaster response except to Carry Out the direct orders of senior management. They are now wholly dependent on *one person* to run the plan.

These plans give employees little to do and hand authority over the disaster response to senior managers alone. They then lay out in great detail procedures and policies but instruct line employees to act like mindless bystanders while management does all the thinking. In my experience, line employees are some of the most capable people on staff and have excellent organizational knowledge. When they aren't mobilized properly, their abilities are wasted.

This problem isn't limited to just businesses. Disaster plans for family residential communities replicate the same mistake. For instance, one of the most common response techniques in community living properties like condo complexes, modular and mobile home parks, and tower apartments is the "captain system." In this system, you have designated individuals who are expected to perform certain activities in the disaster plan on behalf of the residents.

I'll never forget a disaster plan I read in San Diego, California, after an upscale residential community hired me to rewrite its wildfire and earthquake disaster plans. As I approached the office to meet with the community managers for the first time, a man who identified himself as the president of the homeowners' association stepped in front of the door, handed me a thick binder, and said, "I don't know why you were hired, but we don't need you here. We have this under control."

In the binder was one of the most heavy-handed disaster plans I have ever read. There was a significant amount of detail, but, in effect, it said that several first responders, labeled as "captains," lived in the community and would handle all the evacuations on behalf of the other residents. The plan stated that everyone should remain in their homes until given instructions by a captain to evacuate or shelter in place. I'll never forget the last line of the plan: "In the event of a disaster or emergency, the captains will take over the park."

The captains will take over the park? Seriously? I was shocked—it was absolutely ludicrous. The first obvious practical question: What happens if those captains aren't available? What if they are casualties of the disaster and are physically unable to assist? Or what if, during a major natural disaster, the first responders are, you know, working?

The even bigger problem with this plan was that it completely disempowered every resident of the park except the small handful of captains. The implication for residents was clear: *do nothing, and we'll handle it for you.* That is not only insulting to other residents who are perfectly capable of running their own disaster responses, but it also sows seeds of indecision when people are determining what actions to take on behalf of their families. With such a plan in place, no one had any reason to get their own disaster plan and were completely dependent on the captains to handle things for them. In addition, any captains countering the advice of families would increase the general confusion and chaos. The end result: in an emergency, the people affected by this plan would have to rely on someone else and would therefore be forced to become bystanders.

It is important to draw a distinction between "permission" and "notification" as they are written in plans. Notification involves providing information to others in responsible positions about the disaster and is essential in corporate environments. What I object to, however, is when plans require *permission* from those authorities to conduct any kind of disaster response—because preventing almost everyone from executing the plan prevents people from assembling a team or completing any of the time-sensitive, urgent tasks required to address the emergency.

I see this phenomenon with families who use home health companies or other external caregivers to assist a family member with disabilities. When I discuss emergency planning with these families, they often repeat the familiar refrain that the home health company will handle everything for them. The home health company's disaster plan will often make many claims, including that only the company can make arrangements for transportation, sheltering, and food or emergency supplies.

In other words, because an emergency is beyond what they think a disabled person can do alone, *the company will handle everything for them*. I've been hired by large and small home health companies, and I can tell you that this is a fanciful fable. It provides a false sense of security and disempowers people when the company doesn't end up providing families with everything they need in a disaster. Now, of course, a person incapacitated due to mental or physical disability certainly may require someone else to help them. That is what their caregivers are there for. However, this doesn't mean the family should totally surrender control to an outside agency to run the disaster program for them. A disaster plan should be written so that a family can complete important steps without having to leverage an external company.

All of these above situations lead to the same result as in the Hawaiian hotel: a group of perfectly capable people in a permanent state of paralysis, waiting for someone to tell them what to do—bystanders completely dependent on management with nothing to do while nuclear bombs get closer and closer to detonation.

WRITE YOUR DISASTER PLAN LIKE A COOKBOOK FOR SUCCESS

There is a very simple solution to all the above problems. Instead of assuming that someone else will take care of things for you or sifting through a poorly written plan, I want you to start by *writing a disaster plan that assumes that if you do nothing, no one else will, either*. This plan should assume that you are solely responsible for your own disaster response. No captains, no permissions, no paralysis. You take Command, you Communicate, you Carry Out.

The most effective way to do this is to *write your disaster plan like a cookbook*. Yes, a cookbook—with recipes, ingredients, and step-by-step instructions. It should read like one, feel like one, and empower you like one.

This might seem like a strange analogy, but if you think about it, cookbooks are some of the most approachable books in the world. This is because they aren't meant to be just read. They're meant to be *applied*. A really good cookbook is your constant companion as you chop, stir, sauté, boil, grill, and fry. It gives you easily readable instructions and clear directions, beginning with the base ingredients you must collect in the correct quantities. Then it outlines clearly how to prepare those ingredients for cooking, whether you must dice, marinate, or season them. It then lays out exactly how to cook them, with what kind of heat and in what order, while also telling you how to know when a dish is done. But, most importantly, the book doesn't require that you get permission to create the recipes. A cookbook empowers you to prepare virtually any kind of food yourself. It liberates you from any dependency on someone else to make it for you.

Cookbooks also evolve based on the experiences of the cook. My great-grandmother's old cookbook, for example, has olive-oil and tomato-sauce stains and more than a few old crumbs stuck in the binding. In addition, she flagged the book's best recipes—one recipe for banana bread that I grew up on has a smiley face that she drew next to the title. Such evidence of the success of meals past is what makes these books great. When my great-grandmother made changes to the ingredients or found that certain modifications to a recipe would make it better, she noted them in the margins. Your disaster plans should look and feel just like that—minus the stains and crumbs—because disaster plans are designed for *you*.

This is why I don't use long paragraphs with legalistic jargon and technical wording when I write disaster plans. I make sure the plan is easily readable by virtually any audience, and I never write it in a way that disempowers employ-ees. There is a longtime adage in cooking: "All chefs are equal in the eyes of the ingredients." That is the perspective I want you to have when you work on your disaster plan. Any person should be able to pick up the plan and use it.

Sometimes when I'm entertaining guests, I'll pull a book by some celebrity chef, like Rachael Ray. I'll read through it until I find the recipe I want—say, chicken bolognese. And then, Rachael Ray will make me an expert on chicken bolognese. The cookbook tells me exactly what I must do, how I must do it, and how quickly it should be done. The recipe turns me into a cooking star. Your disaster plan should make you a star, too.

C3 METHOD SOLUTIONS

The C3 Method is an ideal system to do just that. With it, you can design your new disaster-plan "cookbook" with "recipes." But instead of chicken bolog-nese, your "recipes" should address wildfires, earthquakes, or acts of terrorism. When correctly applied, the method will help you create a document that will empower you throughout the disaster.

COMMAND - "I CAN EMPOWER MYSELF"

To take Command of creating your disaster plan, you should first reference every disaster plan in your life. When I say "every disaster plan," I mean any plan that has ever affected you in the major areas of your life, whether you wrote it or not. Examples of such areas include:

- Your/your child's school
- Your work
- Your county
- Your utility companies (Electrical, Water, Gas)
- Your apartment/condo/modular community/RV complex

You don't have to read every page (and trust me, you won't want to). You will know in ten seconds if they're any good. Whether you are writing a disaster plan or just evaluating one at your school, your work, or the government—or in any other agency—make sure it is readable. It should use simple, focused language. But a plan has to go further than that to be effective and functional. It can't be written in long paragraphs and use technical legal jargon. That's worse than useless in a disaster: it will slow critical decisions when minutes and seconds can count and will put no confidence in the plan at all. A plan should be written in easy-to-read, short paragraphs, just like you would see in a cookbook. It should also provide clarification on what to do both *during* and *after* a disaster. For example, your workplace's disaster plan must completely address these two questions: Will you be expected to work during a disaster? And if not, will you still be paid? If it doesn't answer these questions, the plan doesn't exist.

When you *evaluate* a disaster plan, if you find that you can't read or understand it, then *assume it doesn't exist.* Assume the one in your hands is nonexistent. Because, in practice, it is—because the chances of it working are close to zero. If you really want to test the language and format of a plan, do what I call the "eighth-grade test" (which is the average reading level in the United States): give your disaster plan to an eighth grader and ask them to explain the first ten steps that they should take in a given disaster based on your plan. If they can't do it, then your plan is overwritten and therefore useless in an emergency.

If you are *writing* a disaster plan, it should expressly say to the person reading it that if they do not act, no one else will, either. It must force the reader to come to the inescapable conclusion that no one else will do anything if they do not act. This is how the plan will combat the Bystander Effect; it will make it clear that this responsibility belongs to them.

Designing your disaster from an empowered mindset in this way takes you from a passive state to an active design state in which you must create your own plans. You will be able to assert your own control over the plans that matter to you by writing and evaluating plans that affect you at home, work, or school. If you find that any of these places don't have a plan in place, then write one yourself. This means you will have a stake in it to make sure it stays up to date and covers the right disasters.

Cookbooks have built this concept directly into the pages. Anyone who opens one up is empowered to follow its instructions because the requirements for each recipe are clearly outlined. That doesn't mean the dish will come out perfectly, but it does mean that I have complete freedom and Command over how the dish is cooked. If I open a Rachael Ray cookbook and find a recipe in there for chicken bolognese, I can guarantee you it won't say, "Call Rachel and wait for instructions."

COMMUNICATE – "I CAN EMPOWER OTHERS"

Remember that while the Command step is about empowering yourself, Communication is about empowering others. Disasters cannot be completely handled alone, which is why your disaster plan must provide the architecture to quickly assemble a custom disaster team. Here is an example:

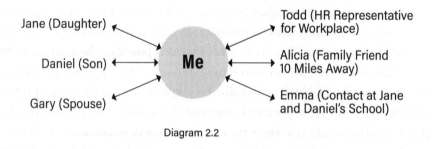

Diagram 2.2

This one is easy: your disaster plan must have a team dynamic written directly into the framework. Anyone should be able to pick it up and then organize a disaster team. In fact, the plan should make this teamwork mandatory. Designing any disaster requires help. Information exchanges not only provide the mechanisms for accessing external information sources but also make it so you can Communicate to others based on the actions you must perform. For example, if your plan addresses a hurricane, it should include mechanisms for receiving information about the storm, as well as for communicating to your loved ones and colleagues if you must evacuate.

In the Disneyland story, I was able to provide clear directions to those around me to ensure that we could respond together as team. I was in Command; however, I was going to need help. And by providing clear directions, I was empowering others to do what was necessary to save that man's life. He was going to need an ambulance, as well as better-equipped responders from the park, which we were able to provide for him through our efficient teamwork. Plans that require endless permissions and authorizations disempower teams and make it nearly impossible for a fluid disaster response to occur.

Your disaster plan must address what kinds of communication mediums are likely to be available in a disaster. For instance, during the 2018 Camp Fire that occurred in Paradise, California, Butte County had such a spike in phone calls that the 911 system became temporarily unavailable. Many do not take advantage of reverse 911 systems available from county and state emergency-management agencies. These systems provide messages from first-response agencies to your phone, informing you of disaster situations. In addition, text messaging is routinely available in disaster areas because the amount of bandwidth required to text is far less than for a regular cell-phone call.

Communication is not just about speaking; it is just as much about listening. Anyone who oversees a disaster response in its initial phases is going to need information from many sources. A disaster plan should empower you to gather such information from as many trusted sources as possible. There shouldn't be any barriers to do so—in fact, you should be encouraged to complete this outreach. This is the lifeblood of any disaster response, as incoming information provides direction for anyone in Command. For instance, in a hurricane, the plan should outline clearly where the reliable sources of information are, such as the Pacific Tsunami Warning Center or the National Weather Service. If these are not outlined, you will be left to rely on almost any source, which may or may not be credible and will affect the important decisions you'll have to make.

CARRY OUT - "WE CAN EMPOWER EACH OTHER"

Disaster plans are valuable tools. They don't have to be complicated or difficult to use—nor should they be. And when written properly, they can make a massive difference in allowing you to design any disaster.

The Carry Out stage is where your disaster plan either succeeds or fails. The steps you lay out must be concise, focused, and 100 percent clear on how to accomplish them.

Cookbooks are tremendously successful when it comes to clear, easy-to-read language. They explain what ingredients you are going to need and in what quantities. Your disaster plan must read the exact same way. If you are going to empower anyone with your plan, then they'll have to be able to read it. Text with excessive jargon is not going to be accessible to most people. Your plan should be concise and simple in its language, with sequential steps, for a clear foundation from beginning to end.

To Carry Out a disaster response effectively, even based on a good plan, there must be resources, supplies, equipment, and even technology that's easily accessible and available. In addition, today's disaster plans tend to get very sophisticated and are situationally dependent. Your team will need much support, which is why plans should allow you and your team to empower each other. For every particular type of incident, you must lay out the exact steps required so that the plan remains manageable and achievable.

Ultimately, if you don't plan, someone else will plan for you, and they will be in full control of your life during a disaster—whether that involves your family, your school, your small business, or even your pets. Develop your own plan. The first page of your disaster plan, whether for family, work, or school, should have simple, easy-to-read steps that clearly outline the tasks to be completed. It must state two main things:

1. **Anyone can use the plan.** Make sure the beginning of the plan actually states this. This sends a clear, unmistakable message that anyone involved in an emergency is instantly empowered to pick up the plan and use it. It needs to be readable and simple to use.
2. **No permissions are needed**. Permission requirements should be eliminated, allowing complete freedom of action for the one in Command. That doesn't mean anyone can just do anything, however. For instance, you may not want your children to turn off the power or your employees to hold a crisis press conference. But basic evacuation, sheltering in place, and lockdowns should be automatic. Use language that bestows leadership so that anyone can allocate roles and manage the initial stages of the disaster response.

Disaster plans are never going to be as exciting as a Harry Potter novel. I totally understand that. But they don't need to be as dull as dishwater, either. Use short, dynamic, actionable language in easy-to-read steps. Graphics and photos should accompany every step, and use lots of colors so the key information stands out clearly.

There should be clear instructions to family members (especially children) on who is appropriate to contact in various circumstances. I see many families who download or purchase premade disaster plans that go on the fridge and list 911 and various other phone numbers, like for poison control and crisis hotlines. These are fine, but they must be accompanied with a disaster plan that lays out clearly when to call which numbers and how to maximize their use. Otherwise, such a list is useless and ignored.

Make sure any family disaster plans you make are easily accessible, such as hanging them on the fridge for everyone to see. You can take a photo of your plan for everyone to reference on their phones. My company developed a mobile app where people can create their own plans very easily because I know they can be time consuming.

Disaster plans must be adaptable, too. My recipe books have notes of things I have learned in making the recipes myself, like different substitutions and changes in the order or execution of steps. Instead of butter, I might use olive oil, or instead of salt, I might opt for a spice that I know will draw out the flavor of whatever I'm cooking. This control allows me to improve the recipe every time I make it. I'm sure Rachael doesn't mind. Your plan should also be flexible to changing conditions. For instance, in our modern society, we deal as much in the virtual world as we do in the brick-and-mortar one. Therefore, you must plan how to account for not only your physical assets (we will discuss this in chapters eight and nine) but also your digital ones. You should create a document that allows your loved ones to access your technology in a disaster if you are unable to do so. This might include passwords or even your cell-phone security code.

Family disaster plans should be written so that anyone can take charge of a disaster. While in longer and more serious disasters that person will likely be an adult, the beginning stages of evacuation, sheltering in place, and lockdown should be something that anyone, including young children, can be self-empowered to get started. If you give children the chance to take some responsibility, they might just surprise you.

I sometimes joke in school presentations that in a disaster, I will take kids over the Army Corps of Engineers any day. They are the ultimate self-starters, and, with a little empowerment, they are surprisingly effective. I was once hired by a school in the Oregon Wine Country to write a plan and teach their teachers and students about the threat of wildfires. As part of the training, I selected two children from each classroom to be responsible for a red emergency backpack containing the disaster plan. I told them they were each responsible for the backpack and, in a disaster, were not to leave the classroom without it.

About a year later, I got a call from the principal, who told me that the school had suffered a minor fire that had required a classroom evacuation. In one of the classrooms, a substitute teacher forgot to bring the emergency backpack. Once they were away from the building and on the grassy yard in the playground, the substitute teacher panicked and tried to go back to get it—until the kids told her that they had gathered it before leaving.

In your family's plan, let your kids have clear responsibilities, like helping to determine when and where to evacuate and helping to gather supplies (see chapters seven and eight).

WRAPPING UP: HAWAII MISSILE ALERT

Ultimately, highly effective disaster plans come down to the successful application of the three elements of the C3 Method: Command, Communicate, and Carry Out. Each of these provides the tools, the resources, and the mindset to empower yourself and those around you in the use of a well-written, current, and actionable disaster plan. Of course, no disaster plan is ever perfect. It should evolve; it should grow; it should empower. When these elements are effectively combined, however, there will be no disaster your plan can't conquer. Likewise, without them, there will be no disaster that can't conquer you.

Hawaii's shock and panic about the nuclear-missile alert came to an end when the state's emergency-management agency admitted that the alert had been sent in error by an employee who had pushed an incorrect button. But before this happened, the manager finally arrived back at the Hawaiian hotel, where chaos, shock, and panic were still well underway. Relieved front-desk workers explained what was going on and asked him where they should send everyone to shelter in place. He turned to them and said, "I don't know. What does the disaster plan say?"

Chapter Three

EQUIPMENT, SUPPLIES, AND TECHNOLOGY THAT ACTUALLY WORK

I was once hired by a group of families at an upscale mobile-home park after delivering a presentation to them. They asked if I would inspect their emergency equipment and determine what else they needed. They stored their equipment and supplies in a garage, each shelf devoted to a different family, with multiple backpacks for each one. One by one, I laid out all the backpacks on a table and reviewed their contents. After going through about a half-dozen of these, I opened a small backpack and was greeted by a black widow spider and a sizable web, jealously guarding the disaster supplies within. Of course, this was a serious problem because anyone putting their hand in there could have certainly received a potentially lethal bite. Had someone quickly opened this bag during a disaster, the lack of access to emergency rooms would have compounded the likelihood of serious injury or death.

While I was a little shocked, this is something that is far too common. Dusty supplies and equipment, outdated first-aid kits—I've seen it all. The culprit in this case: no one had taken responsibility for the backpack . . . or any of the backpacks in the garage, for that matter. The community had simply purchased it, put it in the corner, and believed it would work the instant they needed it. Again, the glorified assumption here is that someone else will design the disaster for you. You buy a pack of supplies and expect it to magically work for you and your family the instant you call on it. However, I must tell you something I've learned from seeing thousands of these situations: disaster supplies, equipment, and technology are not magic wands. They can't do everything for you, even if it's tempting to let them try. Large supplies and fancy gadgets lure you into a false sense of security. In this chapter, I'm going to outline for you the right way to approach equipment so that it decreases your dependence and increases your resilience by turning you into an active responder.

Before we unpack the major problems around disaster supplies and look at how the C3 Method can better prepare us for this element of disaster response, let me define what I mean by Supplies, Equipment, and Technology (EST).

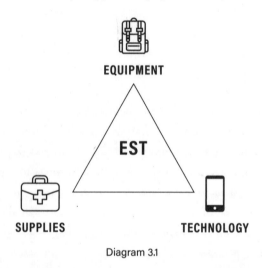

Diagram 3.1

Equipment are tools that can be used and reused in multiple disasters, like flashlights, vests, gloves, etc. *Supplies* are single-use items, like first-aid-kit bandages, batteries, food, water, and other disposables. *Technology* is exactly that: electronic items used to complete a disaster task of some type. This includes software, such as a mobile app, and hardware, such as a mobile hotspot. Typically, equipment and supplies are placed in a backpack or a gym bag and are sealed up for the day when a disaster occurs. While these items can be incredibly helpful, they are typically misused because their purpose within your disaster-response procedures make you more dependent and less prepared than when you didn't have them.

YOU DON'T PURCHASE ANYTHING

The first obvious issue is when you don't collect any EST at all. When you don't buy equipment at all, you are assuming, in effect, that if you do nothing, you will somehow already have everything you need. This means that you are leaving things to chance. Sounds similar to not having a disaster plan at all, doesn't it? You'll have to rely on the government, family members, nonprofits, or first responders—or whatever happens to be lying around in the house—to take care of the situation.

YOU PURCHASE THE WRONG ITEMS

While EST is awesome, it is critical to identify which are right for you because, contrary to popular opinion, not all of it is. Marketing departments have been very effective at convincing people that this or that piece of emergency equipment is the only one you need, even when it isn't.

If you go online for any period of time, you will eventually run into these ads for what I like to call the "wonder weapons" of disaster preparedness: seemingly indestructible flashlights, knives that can cut through the bumper of a car, or a seventeen-part multi-tool that would make MacGyver rethink his trusty old Swiss. I have no problem with these items if they do what they claim, but what does annoy me is when they're marketed to be the only tool you'll ever need for a given task. Most of the time, these wonder weapons overpromise and lull you into a false sense of security. That makes these items not only unhelpful; they actually make you less prepared because you'll feel totally equipped for danger when, in fact, you are just shifting your dependence to an object.

No piece of equipment can do everything for you, and no piece of equipment is *ever* the only flashlight/knife/jacket/etc. you will ever need. Believing otherwise leaves you in a dangerous state of dependence that surrenders your control to some item you bought on the internet. If you want to buy these items, great—but always buy a backup of something else that can perform the same functions as that item does. Remember that equipment and supplies are not useful if you haven't thought through how they will empower you in a disaster. Always consider: What is this stuff doing for you?

Most people do not know if the EST they are acquiring are ones that will fit them correctly. As a result, many people get the wrong items. A good example of this is the ubiquitous red backpack. These backpacks drive me insane for many reasons. First, they are prefilled and zip-tied as an anti-shoplifting measure. This encourages people to never take a look inside of them, which reinforces the assumption that if you do nothing, someone else will do it for you—because you're assuming that the company that packed them did so perfectly and that the backpacks are completely customized to your needs. You are depending on the marketing department of the company that made them to design a disaster on your behalf. This is a big mistake because by doing this, you're basically purchasing your own bystander position.

This is also true for supplies like emergency food and water. Too often, food is bought, put in the corner, and forgotten about. Most of the time, people don't even try the emergency food they purchase. The excuse I generally get is "It's too expensive to waste" or "I don't know how this is going to taste." Well . . . then why did you buy it to subsist off of in a disaster?

I ran into an elderly couple one time who told me they were going to take their RV around the country for eight months and asked if I would go through their onboard supplies. They had one of those red backpacks that they'd bought at a large retailer. It was about the size of a microwave and had been sealed shut with a plastic tie. I agreed to help, so I cut the ties off and dumped all the gear on the table. Among the items were the usual eighty-cent flashlight, a couple of space blankets, yard-work gloves, a whistle, and an item that looked like a hockey puck.

I asked them about the food. They said they had never had it before, so I took a pocketknife I had on me and cut the hockey puck open. Out came what can only be described as a crumbling greenish-brown food pellet. I cut it into two equal parts for the couple. When they asked me what it was, I handed it to them and said, "Lunch. Bon appétit."

After a few awkward seconds, the wife told me that her husband couldn't eat it. She explained that he had celiac disease and couldn't eat gluten, and she wasn't sure what the food pellet contained. So I turned to her and handed her the food to eat. She took one bite and immediately spit it out, saying it tasted terrible to her (I didn't try it myself, as I had already eaten lunch that day). In an emergency where that backpack was their last resort, that food would have been worse than useless to them. It could have made the husband seriously ill, and the wife would have had a hard time keeping the food down.

The problems that equipment and supplies generate are the same for technology. People in our society too often treat technology like it's the solution to every disaster problem. In truth, much of technology leads us to a false sense of security. I see this often with fancy mobile apps and tech gadgets that people purchase.

In terms of software, seemingly every year, I learn of new apps that will "revolutionize" disaster response with everything they promise to do. But a mobile app is a complex system and can have large bandwidth requirements that may not be available after an incident—and you can't test how an app functions during a disaster until a disaster occurs. Will the bandwidth the app takes actually work? Will it do what it promises? These questions linger uncomfortably during a disaster response. This also happens with even well-known platforms. For example, during earthquakes, cell phones often don't work, even though marketing materials from the cell phone company will claim otherwise. And during Hurricane Sandy in 2012, about one in four cell phone towers in the Northeast stopped working, leaving thousands of people unable to make phone calls.[21]

Hardware is arguably worse. I know we all love the latest technology and want to have the best gizmos, but the reality is that most of these—while they work great when the power is working and we have access to good cell towers—often become little more than paperweights in a disaster because our infrastructure hasn't had a chance to catch up to them. Since the 1940s, the Federal Communications Commission has used amateur radio operators, "hams," to provide emergency communications. When I got my amateur radio license, one of the first things I learned was that emergency communications are at the heart of radio. During the chaos of 9/11, most of the established emergency-communication antennas were at the top of the World Trade Center, so licensed hams helped fill the gap.

By blindly believing in what a marketing department advertises, all you're doing is shifting your dependence to technology and making yourself a bystander while gizmos do all the work. You're relying on them to handle your disaster instead of designing your disaster yourself. And if you don't buy anything at all, you're basically relying on the government to handle things through the provision of supplies that may or may not come.

YOU COLLECT TOO MUCH

Overpreparing can be almost as bad as not preparing enough. The main way I see this manifest is when people don't buy equipment that matches the disasters they face. Your disaster response, as you will read in future chapters, is more than simply figuring out how to shower in the dark or getting your cell phone charged. Depending on your profession, the logistics of your life (such as if you are taking care of a vulnerable person or a pet), or your personal beliefs, you might need specialized EST.

When I talk about gathering items in preparation for a disaster, I inevitably get questions about the "prepper lifestyle." Let me give a basic background on this. The movement is really an offshoot of survivalist preparation that rose to prominence in the early 1990s after the first Gulf War. "Preppers" focus on self-reliance, self-sufficiency, and the importance of taking care of yourself in preparation for cataclysmic disasters.[22]

I love these folks because I applaud their philosophy of individual preparedness and initiative. There is no group of people who better exemplify the assumption that if they do nothing, no one else will, either. They challenge you to think proactively and not to surrender control of your disaster response to anyone. Their lifestyle prioritizes compiling equipment and supplies for major national emergencies, particularly catastrophic ones in which the national infrastructure is compromised and traditional social safety nets are eliminated. As a result, preppers gather large stockpiles of food, water, and survivalist tools to prepare for significant time off the grid.

Pursuing this lifestyle is fine as long as you do so with a healthy mindset. First, you need to realize that most disasters obviously aren't apocalyptic—or even close to it. Hollywood films routinely mislead people in this respect. That means there can easily be an overreaction to minor emergencies, which can create a dangerous temptation toward panic and can skew rational decision-making. For instance, if you have a prepper stash, just make sure it doesn't tempt you to stay home when it would be safer to evacuate. For those who live in rural areas without many modern infrastructure and logistics, prepper stashes can be a terrific advantage. This doesn't mean they are appropriate for everyone, however.

In addition, survivalist skills that are an inimical part of the prepper lifestyle are also fine to learn, particularly if you live in a rural area. However, if you live in an urban area, make sure you aren't overemphasizing outdoor-style skills, like learning to improvise a fishing rod and line or making a rabbit snare from twigs (yes, I learned how to do this once from my Wilderness EMT instructor), over the practical skills that will serve you well in areas with modern infrastructure.

Disaster equipment and supplies are valuable, but only if you have the right ones. Too often I see organizations value quantity over quality and make purchases without considering real-life applications. I remember when a school hired me to run a full-scale disaster drill. This particular school boasted that it was the most prepared in the entire state. As part of the planning process, I went to look at its equipment and supply bin. What I found there I can honestly say I hadn't seen in all my years of being an emergency manager. It was filled to the brim with every conceivable tool and supply you could imagine. There were chemical toilets, showers, backboards, shovels, and a huge container for medical supplies. The bin was even equipped with a portable suture kit. The school probably could have set up a field hospital.

However, when I read its disaster plan, I noticed something: it said that in a disaster, the school wouldn't even house the kids overnight—students would almost immediately be sent home. The school leadership, in concert with the district, had determined that students must be evacuated within eight hours of a disaster. In addition, the school was in one of the wealthiest areas in the country. It was not the kind of place where you're going to need chemical showers for children. It became clear that when the equipment was purchased, the school hadn't realized how useless most of it would be. In fact, as I was completing the training for the staff on the disaster plan, I decided to take a poll on who knew how to suture a wound. Not a single hand was raised.

YOU BUY IT AND FORGET ABOUT IT

But let's say you've found the cool piece of disaster equipment you want, and you decide to buy it. Once you take it home, we all know what's going to happen next: it's going to be a subject of family conversation for, say, five minutes, and then over the next five days there will be a debate as to where it should go—and then you'll stick it in the corner, waiting for the next flood. Until then, spiders will make it their home. You're not going to test the equipment. It's not coming out of that bag. I mean, why would you take it out of its beautiful packaging?

Flashlights, knives, mobile apps, and emergency supplies will not work for you unless you put them through a serious test of usefulness. But most of the time, that doesn't happen. In addition, when your EST aren't maintained, their usefulness degrades very quickly. They collect dust and not much else.

By leaving the backpacks intact and unexamined, you're actually making yourself far *less* prepared because you're assuming—falsely, in some cases—that they're going to work. No one will be assigned responsibility for the supplies. No one will maintain them. No one will care about them. No one will be empowered around EST preparedness. And disaster equipment that is not properly maintained is virtually useless. You increase your reliance on it, but you never test it.

This is dangerous—assuming the infomercial's claims are fully correct, for instance, when the reality is that you don't know if the items you bought are going to work. You might not even know if all the items advertised were actually included in your purchase. And those items certainly won't care for themselves. Are there batteries in the flashlights? What's the expiration date and ingredients on the rations? And so on.

Then, when there's a power outage three years later, someone will ask, "Didn't we buy a disaster backpack or something?" and stumble in the dark to locate it. And when you find it, you will demand everything inside it to perform like on the day you bought it. But that's not how it works. EST must be maintained. They erode and expire.

I think sometimes people feel as though their EST are meant to completely prevent a disaster when all they can do is act as a problem solver. I love watching murder-mystery television, including a show called *Banacek*, starring George Peppard, that ran in the early 1970s. Peppard plays a private detective who always seems to have an "old Polish proverb" at the ready whenever he needs some guidance on a clue or a witness. One that has stuck with me whenever I think about EST is this: "Twelve good horses and silver candlesticks won't stop the snow from falling in Bialystock."[23] What he's trying to impart in that TV wisdom—I think—is that even the best technology and gadgets can't stop the forces of Mother Nature; they can only help you manage them.

C3 METHOD SOLUTIONS

COMMAND - "I CAN EMPOWER MYSELF"

Disaster EST can be incredibly useful to you if you take the right approach to them. But if you treat them like magic wands, they are guaranteed to disappoint you. The better approach is to view them as part of your team, which will decrease your dependency on them. I want you to consider every EST you buy like it's a cooking tool you can use to follow the disaster "recipes" of wildfires, blizzards, or tornadoes. The utensils won't cook the food for you; you have to take command of them.

You must take Command of EST by totally changing your approach to them. Acquire equipment, supplies, and technology on the basis of this assumption alone: you are the one fully responsible for sourcing the right EST.

Assuming limitations will force you to plan contingencies and truly test your supplies, taking you from a passive state to an active design state. You'll be relying on your own action and problem-solving abilities instead of a clever marketing campaign to tell you what you need in a disaster. This will allow you to assert control over your own disaster equipment. You can determine your own level of dependence. For every piece of EST, ask yourself, "Does this increase my dependence on something I can't control?"

For instance, I hear many people tell me that as long as they have a generator, they're fine. No plans needed. The generator will create electricity, which means they can charge their phones, walk around without a flashlight, and keep their ice cream intact during an emergency. What they do not realize is they have now handed their disaster response to a piece of equipment. This is a single point of failure. You're no longer in charge of whether your disaster response will be successful. Nope—that's now the job of the machine outside. Instead, make your generator just one of many (at least three) strategies in your disaster response to provide you with light, power, and refrigerated food.

COMMUNICATE - "I CAN EMPOWER OTHERS"

Transform your EST into members of your team. They should work with you and assist you with tasks you can't complete on your own, but they can't take over. Learn what your inventory can and can't do, just like if you were recruiting a member of a team. Here is what a good team looks like when you consider the equipment and supplies:

Diagram 3.2

I have arranged these items this way to illustrate that you are the center of the team, while everything around you should provide you with a particular skill. The EST is just one member of your team. They aren't the team itself, and they won't do everything for you. I love this analogy because in it, you are the chef. You make the food. The utensils provide a basic skill but are totally inanimate without you. When this is done properly, you'll still be able to make decisions on your own, and your EST will serve you in the way and manner you need.

You should also have backup EST that vary slightly in purpose. For instance, in my home, I have a full block of knives. Among them, I have a chef's knife, a serrated knife, paring knives, vegetable knives, and even a knife called a santoku that I use to cut dense cheeses or chop vegetables in a hurry. However, even that knife can't do everything, nor would I expect it to.

You shouldn't expect your EST to do everything, either. For example, no matter where you live or what disasters you face, you *must* have flashlights. Notice that I made that plural. Much like my knives, there is no one flashlight that can do everything. When I work with clients, I tell them they need three kinds of flashlights:

- One that lights your living areas (a larger, wide-strobe flashlight)
- One that helps you see as you move around (a miner's helmet flashlight)
- One to illuminate items both close and far (a sturdy hand flashlight)

So instead of trying to buy some flashlight that claims to do everything, get one of each. That way, you'll have one that can light up your house, one that you can use as you walk around as you normally would, and one for when you need to search in the garage for something. If all three tasks are being done by one flashlight, then you are wholly dependent on it to do everything. You are surrendering control of your surroundings to a single point of failure. That flashlight isn't on your team. That flashlight *runs* the team. Instead, by having multiple backups tailored to specific roles, you can maintain control of your disaster response and not surrender it to a piece of equipment.

CARRY OUT – "WE CAN EMPOWER EACH OTHER"

Now that you have your team, you have to empower it to be successful. To fully apply the C3 Method to EST, there is a simple three-step process I want you to apply to every item you buy.

1. Buy it.
2. Try it.
3. Don't rely on it.

This will give you a healthy relationship to disaster supplies. It's easy to blindly believe marketing materials—that's part of how marketing and advertising words. But it's important to push back against those claims and do your own due diligence. You, not some company's marketing department, are the one designing your disaster, after all. So crack open that backpack. Better yet, determine what you actually need and then acquire your EST piece by piece.

These three actions should guide you to a place where you are taking responsibility and realizing the limitations of your EST. Items you are using should have a clear expectation of use, not taking over everything. This process will also help you identify missing items. People forget to buy fresh items all the time, but they also forget to gather their personal documents and belongings during a disaster. Many of the critical items you will need in a major disaster aren't things that you can just buy in a store. For instance, after Hurricane Katrina, many people had trouble because they had lost their identification and couldn't get verified for many services.[24] Examples of these critical items include papers, prescriptions, and personal and priceless items, which we'll cover in further detail in chapter eight.

Buy It

Start by purchasing an *empty* backpack (like a large outdoor backpack) that will hold everything you need. Comfort is important, so try it on. It should also have multiple pouches. Don't *ever* buy a prefilled backpack that hasn't been customized to you. Once you've purchased your empty backpack, buy items to place inside of it.

What should you put in your backpack? It depends. But I can help you come to your own answers. If you have a disaster plan, rely on that to determine what your EST needs are. If you don't have a plan, it will be more difficult to truly customize it to you—but certainly not impossible. In any case, go to the store and handpick your needed EST. Don't be fooled by marketing hype. There's nothing worse than EST that don't work in a disaster. Lives may be on the line. You must get equipment that matches what your lifestyle is and what you'll actually need in a real disaster. Well-written disaster plans can help with this, but a thoughtful examination of your life can also help. Never buy an item that says "the only ____ you need" without getting backups.

That doesn't mean you must have three knives, three gloves, and three first-aid kits. Focus on tasks before numbers. Instead of thinking about how many knives to buy, ask yourself, "What do I need a knife to do?" You'll need it to cut things, but what exactly will you cut? Food? Rope? Tarps? Clothing? It depends entirely on what your disaster plans say and what kinds of threats you are facing. Depending on your answer, I'd suggest acquiring backups like scissors, a steak knife, a razor blade, or a box cutter. But say you have one knife that "does it all"—in a disaster, do you really want the knife you just used to cut some old rope or a roll of duct tape to then chop your food? This task-based thinking is what I want you to focus on as you buy EST.

Once you have taken this inventory, I want you to buy a backpack for each member of your family. Write their names on each one and make it clear that the equipment and supplies in there are for them only. I do this with my own backpack; my emergency backpack at home is embroidered with my own name, and all the supplies contained within belong to me. This makes it 100 percent clear that I am responsible for making sure that my equipment and supply backpack works specifically for the tasks I need completed and prioritized.

For example, I am very particular about the kind of food I want to eat in a disaster. Therefore, the emergency food I have stocked follows the precise menu I have designed for myself. I have dried beef stroganoff, grilled cheese sandwiches, and chicken bolognese (yes, I like this dish). Food can make a big difference in my morale, as it can for you, too. Fill your backpack with food that reflects this.

While I may not know exactly what you need, there are a few must-haves. Since no disaster book is complete without an equipment list, here is a *basic* one. This list is *not comprehensive* but is enough to be a baseline.

Equipment	Supplies	Technology
Heavy Gloves	Duct Tape	Cell-Phone Charger
Rope	Batteries	Weather App
Multipurpose Tool	First-Aid Kit	Local Emergency
Flashlight (Wide)	Basic Food	Management App
Flashlight (Miner)	Water Packets	Laptop Charger
Flashlight (Hand)	Space Blanket	
Can Opener	Yellow Chalk	
Safety Glasses	Dust Mask	

Before you buy any item, recognize the limitations of it. You may have noticed that fire extinguishers have a series of letters on them: A, B, C, D, and K. Each letter represents a classification of a type of fire they can extinguish, like wood, electrical, or chemical fires.[25] Most household ones (like the one in my home) are ABC extinguishers, which is fine because that covers most types of fires that the average person will likely encounter. However, in a commercial facility or in industrial areas, an ABC extinguisher would be inappropriate and insufficient for the types of fires you would likely face there. One fire extinguisher can't do everything; different fire extinguishers put out different kinds of fires. Don't buy things that don't fit what you are planning to do.

I'll never forget this nursing-home client I had in Minnesota. They showed me their emergency-supply closet, and, like clockwork, my eyes set on a strange shape. It was in this large canvas bag. The person I was with didn't know what was inside, so I asked them if they would pull whatever it was out of the bag. I kid you not: it was an inflatable raft. And what's even better was that I found paddles for it in the back of the storage room.

I later asked the administrator what the purpose was for the raft, and she told me that since the facility was next to a major river, they could possibly use that to evacuate residents quickly. That conversation was almost a decade ago, and I still can't figure out how that would have been accomplished with elderly residents, many of whom were not even fully cognizant of their surroundings, let alone ambulatory.

Try It

You must try your equipment out! If you are a school or business, run a drill with the equipment. Take it out of the plastic and give it a spin! Eat the food; drink the drinks. Don't just assume you are going to be willing to eat the food in a disaster. You would be amazed at what is edible and drinkable. A 1957 experiment conducted by the Atomic Energy Commission demonstrated that beer is actually safe to drink after an atomic blast. While beer bottles would be radioactive, their contents would not (although the flavor would be slightly altered).[26]

Turn the generator on (yes, with gas). You may discover that you'll need training on its use. So make sure you read whatever instruction manuals you have and learn how your EST work. When I was a young professional, I had a unique opportunity to be trained in chemical-weapon response with VX nerve agent at the Center for Domestic Preparedness in Anniston, Alabama. One of the things I distinctly remember about the experience is the fit training they had us do to ensure that our masks contoured exactly to our faces so no external air would get inside. And they didn't take our word for it. There were machines that made sure the fit was perfect, having us move our arms and head around to check for breaches in the mask fit. You couldn't even start the training until your mask had been fully fit tested. This is the kind of approach you must take with your EST.

Once you gather all your EST, I want you to first set up accountability for your equipment. Start by laying it all out. Collect every piece of emergency equipment and first-aid kit—the works—and put it all in a pile. If you already bought the red backpack, no worries. Unzip it, turn it upside down, and shake it until it's empty (don't forget the side pockets). Take any items you find out of the plastic and add them to the pile. Now, test everything to make sure it works. Test every flashlight. Check and make sure that nothing is expired. This is the only way to start. If you have food, make sure it works for you! If you have gluten allergies, you don't want to eat the pellet in the hockey puck—then you'll be ill throughout the disaster. Get food that makes sense for you. When it comes to first-aid kits, you don't have to test them—but make sure all the expiration dates are still good.

For each family member, put everything they will need into their individual backpack, leaving one pouch empty (we'll talk about what to put there in chapter eight). Then, set up any technological tools you may have. Don't download new apps during a disaster. Do it now. Don't use gizmos unless their technology has been proven in another disaster.

Don't Rely On It

When I say this, I don't mean that you should never rely on your EST. What I mean is that you shouldn't rely on them exclusively. They're like any other material items: they can break or just stop working. If you make the assumption that you can't rely on them, then you won't *over-rely* on them to do everything for you.

With any EST, I want you to start with the assumption that it *doesn't work*. While this might seem contradictory, it's actually a healthy mindset to have around EST because it recognizes and assumes their limitations. It forces you to closely examine your items and take responsibility for them.

If done properly, you're going to realize that your equipment has limits and requires individual initiative to make it work. During Hurricane Gustav in 2008, I was a shelter manager for the American Red Cross. While looking over the equipment and supplies we were given to get the shelter going, I literally took everything out. Alongside two other volunteers, I checked every cot, every blanket, every pillow to make sure that nothing was damaged. Although the equipment had already been reviewed by others, we didn't make any assumptions and tested them ourselves. In doing so, we discovered a number of items that were damaged or unusable.

Relying on equipment you haven't fully tested is a serious mistake. I used to work as a consultant to an environmental marine company, and I once had to evacuate a number of beachfront coastal work areas where employees were performing environmental cleanup work during the BP oil spill. At one of the sites, I had the supply vendor deliver emergency equipment and supplies, but I locked them up because the supplies were for drills and training only and were all intentionally expired and/or damaged. I told all the employees about the supplies and figured nothing would happen. I was wrong. The dock manager, disregarding my instructions, took bolt cutters and cut the padlocks off to get at them. When I arrived at the site, he had already opened the supplies and was using them, even though there were perfectly good first-aid kits elsewhere.

We all love our cell phones and tech gizmos, but in a disaster, you must recognize their limitations. We all know that technology isn't perfect, so don't treat it like a magic wand. Don't use experimental software unless it has been tested and proven to be reliable *in* a disaster.

I once made a disaster plan for an outdoor resort in Yosemite, California. It had breathtaking views and a river that ran through the middle of the park. As I was writing the plan, the management told me that they were going to rely solely on cell phones for communicating with one another. I thought this was interesting because my phone (which was top-of-the-line at that time) was barely getting one bar of reception there, and I'd had times when I couldn't hear someone during a call. So I decided to put it to the test and asked the manager to send an employee to the farthest end of the park and have them call me on my phone. The employee returned thirty minutes later, explaining that there'd been no reception.

You should also be wary of disaster mobile apps. I love some of these apps, and, in fact, I have a disaster app of my own. When people download Disaster Hawk®, they are often shocked at how simple it is, with very few frills. This is done intentionally—simple search functions and streamlined, shareable plans. I did this because I see so many disaster apps that have complex communication functionalities, with sophisticated alerts and messaging functions and every-thing else, and then I find out they don't work well in disasters because they require a lot of bandwidth. I have discovered a rule that I want you to keep in mind: *the fancier the app, the less likely it will work in a disaster.*

With supplies, remember that they have an expiration date. They aren't going to last forever, and you must assume that they could expire by the time you start to use them. Check at least a few of them, and if they are dried up or compromised, buy new ones.

WRAPPING UP: THE SPIDER THAT NEVER BIT

Equipment, Supplies, and Technology (EST) are critical team members in your disaster-preparedness program. From masks to first-aid kits to flashlights to mobile apps, they can provide you with a tremendous advantage in virtually any disaster. However, when you allow them to become cure-alls by depending too much on them, they can become a tremendous weakness. If you use the C3 Method—and remember that you must "buy it, try it, and not rely on it"—you will put yourself in a position to maximize their effectiveness to design any disaster. Because if your EST isn't able to empower you, then I guarantee you they're going to eventually house a black widow spider, much like the bag I encountered in that mobile-home park.

When I saw the spider, I instinctively recoiled, dropping the backpack on the counter, realizing suddenly that I had come within a few inches of being bitten. Once I had reset myself, I took a hard look at the backpack to make sure the creature hadn't come crawling out.

As I inspected the backpack, I noticed that it was very distinctive in its design. It was a Little Mermaid backpack with the name "Lilly" written with a heart for the dot over the "i." It was much smaller than the other backpacks and had been lovingly packed. In fact, as I collected myself and closed the bag, I noticed that a copy of Lilly's birth certificate had fallen out. That was when I discovered: the person who would have opened this backpack was a four-year-old girl.

Part Two

REACT

Seize Control Seconds After Disaster Strikes with the C3 Method

Chapter Four

PRACTICE LIKE IT'S THE REAL THING

I was once hired by a school that asked me to evaluate a disaster drill it was going to run. It told me that it was the most disaster-prepared primary school in the state and challenged me to find anything wrong with its preparedness. The drill's fake scenario was a massive earthquake that disrupted the network of roads around the school, so students would have to stay in the building overnight. The school asked me to evaluate its procedures and policies as if the situation were real.

One of the things the school showed me was its equipment trailer, which contained most of the supplies that would be used during the drill. One of these items was a manual portable generator the school planned to use for external lighting. This was a critical piece of equipment, as the fake scenario called for an overnight stay. When the drill started, I asked staff about the generator, telling them they needed to start it for me. They refused, telling me, "Oh, we don't do that. It's too much trouble, loading it with gas and all that." I suddenly took a hard look at the generator and noticed something funny: not only had it never been turned on, but they also hadn't even removed the price tag!

Disaster drills and training are, without question, the most important readiness activities you can perform. When conducted properly, they provide a realistic sense of disaster conditions and allow you to identify weaknesses in your disaster program. It can be a sobering experience when you make a good disaster plan; buy all the latest equipment, supplies, and tech gizmos you need; and then run a training or drill and realize that the plan completely flopped, the equipment didn't work, the supplies are outdated, and the tech failed. But I tell people, "Great! Better to know *before* the disaster!" That's why these activities are so valuable. But not all are the same. There are too many that do not live up to expectations.

First, let me define "drills" and "training"—it is important to realize that they are *not* the same thing. Training is a process of familiarizing yourself with how plans, equipment, and supplies will work in a disaster. A drill, however, involves trying everything under realistic conditions. Each of these plays a critical part in your disaster-preparedness program because each reinforces critical behaviors in a disaster.

TRAINING IS INEFFECTIVE

The first major problem I see with most training is that they don't come close to adequately preparing trainees for a real disaster. Training is when you learn how you will operate in a disaster, whether it's a disaster affecting your family, your school, or your work. It should provide you with all the skills you need to successfully execute a disaster response. However, most of the time, trainings cover topics that completely disempower you from responding effectively to a disaster. For instance, I was hired by a home health company in Pennsylvania that, prior to my arrival, told employees that in the event of a disaster where they were in a client's home, they were to sit in their cars and do nothing until contacted by a supervisor. They had each been given a tablet to use that housed all their software and would provide them with emergency information. However, what I discovered was that many of the tablets were being used in areas with almost no data coverage. In other words, they were in "dead zones"! That meant that in practice, employees would never receive the right disaster information and would get absolutely zero leadership. This disempowered every single employee and rendered the company's training absolutely useless.

Not only is training often disempowering, but it also usually isn't detailed enough. Presenters go chapter and verse into how to respond in the first few seconds or minutes of a disaster—and that's it. They never discuss with you how to take control during a disaster, how to deal with a company's recovery, or how to lead a team when an emergency is occurring. These are important especially if paychecks are involved. COVID-19 shocked people because they realized that they had zero training on recovery and continuity.

This common practice subtly reinforces the "Do nothing, and we'll take care of you" narrative. You'll continue to rely on others and will assume that someone else will handle your disaster response since the presenters you listen to don't seem to think you need additional knowledge and training. The silent message is clear: "Who cares? You're not going to be doing anything, anyway."

Many times, however, trainings face the opposite problem of being *too detailed*. Countless trainings I've seen cover topics that people don't need and are never going to remember. This results in mind-numbingly boring presentations. Most of the time, when talking about a disaster plan, presenters try to teach people every little action. Go here. Go there. Do this. Do that. For instance, in Florida, I often see organizations running hurricane trainings. They'll talk about what they're going to do at ninety-six hours before landfall, seventy-two hours before landfall, then forty-eight hours before landfall. Yawn. Nobody cares about that, and they are never going to remember. It ends up being a waste of time for everyone.

I have been an internationally award-winning speaker and trainer for over twenty years, earning a Teaching Excellence Award from the Department of Homeland Security, and I have trained tens of thousands of people. I can tell you with confidence that audiences fall asleep to these kinds of presentations. This leaves you dangerously underprepared for a disaster and not equipped to face an actual incident, particularly ones that strike suddenly and with great force. In effect, it would've been better to not do the training at all.

DRILLS ARE INEFFECTIVE

Once you train, disaster drills are the next stage. This is your chance to learn what's working well and what's not. The problem is that most drills and exercises I have observed are no better than trainings at preparing you for real disaster conditions. I can zero in on the one major flaw in almost 99 percent of all drills I encounter: they're scripted. The drill I see done almost all the time is what I call the "Shakespeare drill." You know what I'm talking about. It's a hyper-choreographed drill where everyone knows their lines, where to stand, and when to enter and exit the stage. Everything runs exactly on schedule. In other words, it's nothing like a real disaster.

Schools are the worst offenders when it comes to this kind of drill. Here is how this Shakespearian farce plays itself out:

....

Characters in the Play

MONICA, the *Principal*

ROSS
CHANDLER   *The Teachers*
PHOEBE
RACHEL

JANICE   *Students*
JOEY

<Scene 1>

Enter Monica on the public address system.

MONICA   All students, teachers, staff—attend to me.
                A drill is taking place. Evacuate!

All characters leave their rooms in an orderly fashion. Teachers enter the field stage left with the students, and Monica the Principal enters stage right.

MONICA   I've lost my whistle! Must have my whistle now!
CHANDLER   Right here! I found your whistle here!
MONICA   My vest! I need my reflective vest right now!
PHOEBE   Well, here you are. Your vest was safe with us.

ROSS   And here's your clipboard. Take it from me and run.

The teachers conduct a roll of the students and send to Monica. The students
are chewing gum, laughing, and pulling up the grass. They're having a good
time, talking with their friends until it's time to back inside. Joey is now placing
grass in Janice's hair while her back is turned to get her attention.

JANICE   You have to stop it, Joey! You're so annoying.

JOEY   So, how you doin'? How you doin', girl?

RACHEL   Oh, Joey, you're hassling Janice again—just come!

MONICA   Okay, we're done. Good job to all. Let's go.

Monica uses her whistle, and everyone exits stage right.

End.

....

This script plays out in drills time and time again, with barely anything learned from them. In this example, Monica does most of the work, dictates the direction of the story, and is the only important character. Everyone else is just a side character or comic relief.

The problem with these drills is that they don't accurately reflect what a real disaster is like in a way that would make them valuable as serious examinations of an organization's disaster preparedness. First, they're completely predictable. If you read through *Hamlet*, you can watch a production of the play and know exactly what is going to happen, when it will happen, and who's going to do what. That's great for Shakespeare, but it's terrible when it comes to disaster preparedness because real disasters aren't predictable or the same every time. When I observe Shakespeare drills, I like to have some fun with the participants—without so much as picking up a piece of paper or turning on my phone, I can come up with a dozen scenarios that would easily turn their script into chaos.

Not only are the conditions within a Shakespeare drill not realistic, but its tempo is also entirely inaccurate. Usually, these drills run at a hurried pace—but not the frenetic one that would inevitably accompany any attempt to evacuate a group of six- to ten-year-olds when a building is shaking, on fire, or terrorized by a person with a gun.

These drills are also boring. Nothing interesting ever happens. In a professional setting, you drag your feet to a mandatory drill, say hi to your colleagues, and then text apologies to your coworkers for running late to your next meeting, wondering why in the world you've wasted your day with such a pointless activity. It's no wonder that no one really ends up taking these drills seriously. Not only do they turn everyone into passive lemmings, but they also reinforce the Bystander Effect, granting full responsibility to a handful of people while everyone else is subtly told to stand around and do nothing. This destroys a golden opportunity to empower people with leadership responsibility in a disaster, squandering it by turning people into bystanders who are not learning or getting anything out of these drills.

LESSONS ARE NEVER LEARNED FROM THE DRILLS

Even when drills are run (whether effectively or not), they never have their valuable lessons captured and incorporated into plans. Every drill or exercise that you run must have their lessons learned, captured, and later incorporated into your disaster plan. In disaster drills I observe, I rarely read accompanying notes that are worth incorporating into disaster plans. The ones I most often see are normally just silly bits of data that don't mean anything, like what time the drill started and stopped, what the weather was, or the name of the person taking notes. I also sometimes encounter notes like this one from a drill I saw in Ohio: "Drill was successful. Everyone did perfectly." Who ran this drill? Joy from the Disney movie *Inside Out*? There is no such thing as "perfect" in a drill. Even when I was a drama kid reciting soliloquies from Shakespeare, I made mistakes in performance—and that was when there was no one else on stage! Again, these kinds of notes lack meaning because they don't contain teachable or actionable information and don't provide places to grow and improve around the disaster response.

What this means is that people are running the drill but not learning anything from it. If there aren't real suggestions offered by it, the act itself of running the drill is pointless. No one will take responsibility for the drill, and the lessons that were there but never documented will dissolve into the ether. The reason this happens is because, in drills, a few leaders take over and everyone else becomes useless. No need to learn anything; we've got this. This implies and reinforces that someone else will do things for you. You will therefore repeat the same mistakes in drill after drill. And when lessons are not properly incorporated from drills into plans, your drills will actually make you less prepared than without them because they will reinforce poor behavior and entrench the poison of the Bystander Effect.

C3 METHOD SOLUTIONS

I want your training and drills to be something special. They should be experiences that explore every avenue of your disaster program and reinforce the power of individual responsibility, which can transform participants into an elite emergency response team. The C3 Method provides you with a comprehensive blueprint to run drills that will actually expose the weaknesses in your disaster preparedness and at the same time empower people with leadership and confidence.

In high school, I was a drama kid, and during my senior year, I performed in a production of *West Side Story*, a musical set in 1960s New York. It's a modern rendering of Shakespeare's *Romeo and Juliet*. If you haven't had the opportunity to see one, a musical essentially has three elements to it: dialogue, singing, and dancing. *West Side Story* is unique in that not only are there are a *minimum* of thirty characters in it (usually closer to forty or fifty with ensemble background characters), but there are also times when large numbers of them sing and dance *simultaneously* onstage. You can't imagine the controlled chaos on that stage unless you've been a part of it. A significant amount of coordination is required so that actors do not run into one another and are in the correct positions at the beginning and the end of the scenes.

What I would like you to do is convert your training and drills from *Romeo and Juliet* to *West Side Story*. Stop pretending like disasters involve two people onstage exchanging soliloquies—instead, run your drills with dozens of people all onstage, moving, talking, singing, and dancing at the same time. It will give you a sense of the real chaos you would experience in an actual incident.

When I first began my *West Side Story* rehearsals, the cast went through the scenes together, out of order from easiest to hardest, reading the script and practicing the song lyrics. The priority was to just learn the lines and make sure that everyone knew the songs and learned the basic dance choreography. However, as we got closer to opening night and ran through the scenes sequentially, we realized something: the logistics were a mess. But a good mess—better to figure that out in rehearsal than during the live performance. In one scene, for instance, a cast member needed to leave on one side of the stage, and in the next one, they had to be on the opposite side and hold a prop carried by another character in a separate area of the stage, making an exchange nearly impossible.

That prop problem is an obvious one you can't identify when scenes are rehearsed out of order. After all, it is only when you blend together the script (disaster plan), the props (equipment and supplies), the sets and lighting (technology), and the singing and choreography (training) during a full dress rehearsal (disaster drill) that you'll see how certain things that looked great on the drawing board will need to be modified based upon actual conditions. Because on opening night (the disaster), things work much more smoothly when all of these run in synchronization. And after the live performance is over, there are blocking and choreography fixes (post-disaster reports).

There is no way I can describe to you the rush, nerves, and sheer adrenaline of opening night. It's never perfect. There is always something to work on, but the intense focus everyone applies to their own performance makes for a great show.

COMMAND - "I CAN EMPOWER MYSELF"
The drills and training you run must reinforce individual empowerment; otherwise, they are virtually useless. In real disaster situations, you must be prepared for instances where the people who are in charge become incapacitated, go off-site, or are just unavailable. In fact, I want you to take this a step further—instead of assuming that leadership will be available, in every training and drill *I want you to assume no one can be in charge but you.* That's right. This will make it impossible for you to fall into the Bystander Effect trap. You must lead. That means you must read the plan, you must find and use the EST, and you will have to make the technology gizmos work.

Taking Command should be a critical goal of your drills and training programs. They should rotate leadership responsibilities and diffuse out the roles so that every single person in your organization or community understands that they are either going to be part of the solution or part of the problem. Once you do that, I guarantee that every person will be awake during training, whether people in your family, your school, or your small business. I have seen it myself; when people are given responsibility over the disaster response, they step up and demonstrate incredible leadership ability. You can't institute a program that disenfranchises people; participants will always default to the Bystander Effect if you build it into your program.

If you have a child in school, you must not only learn their school's disaster plan, but you should also be directly involved in at least one of the school's drills. One of the biggest issues in disaster response for school leadership is when parents don't understand what's going on and teachers and school administrators get into shouting matches with them during a real evacuation. I'm sure you can picture it: Lines of cars filled with anxious parents who have one priority—to get their child. Parents suddenly abandoning their cars and running up to the school to grab their children as quickly as possible. Teachers trying to protect children from being taken by an unauthorized adult. It's a recipe for a serious security problem.

If you're going to design a disaster, you can't just say that you're going to empower leaders. You must accurately simulate it. My fire drills are unique because I run them in ten-minute increments. We do the entire drill in ten minutes, and then we do it again. And again. And again. And each time, I put a different person in charge.

I'm convinced that drills need to force all participants into a place of individual initiative and must seriously challenge how they would respond to a disaster. Every drill you either participate in or organize must require everyone to take individual responsibility for the group's disaster response.

COMMUNICATE - "I CAN EMPOWER OTHERS"

During any real disaster, where there is chaos and confusion, organizing a team is critical. Therefore, your drills must simulate organizing teams under realistic conditions. Training should do likewise. This forces people out of being reactive and teaches them to be proactive instead. The drills must empower people to work in an unstable environment within teams. That way, you can simulate real teamwork and grow leadership between people who may have to work together in a real disaster. This is what a team might look like:

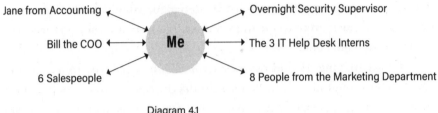

Diagram 4.1

You might notice that this chart includes many strangers. This is intentional; drills should encourage people who rarely or never work together to collaborate as direct team members. For example, I ran a disaster drill with a big home health company in Michigan. One of the offices I was working at had a call center, home health agents, executive offices, and much more. When I ran their drill, I deliberately grouped people who had never worked together before to form the disaster team. They had to learn to communicate and cooperate in a new way to effectively get tasks completed. I've also placed first responders on here because if you can incorporate them into your drills, you should.

CARRY OUT – "WE CAN EMPOWER EACH OTHER"

Training

Training should make it clear that everyone is responsible for the disaster response. To do this, make sure that basic skills are learned first. Train so that these skills become automatic. Training should be fun—but what I call "focused fun." Keep in mind that training doesn't have to involve rote memorization; returning to the analogy from chapter two, remember that good disaster plans are like cookbooks with recipes that can be clearly followed by anyone.

Can—and should—only one person do all the cooking? Absolutely not. Anyone can cook the dish if they are familiar with the basic skills of cooking. Really effective disaster training provides those skills so that anyone can pick up the "recipe book" and use it, even if they have never seen it before.

Do cookbooks require a certain amount of training? Absolutely. I mean, you need to know how to sauté things. You have to know what it means to blanch a vegetable, or mince it, or dice it (I learned the hard way that there's a difference between mincing and dicing). Cooking is made much more efficient when you have these skills. Likewise, there are certain practices and techniques during a disaster response that must be differentiated and learned. But you don't have to teach every recipe from start to finish. That is why you have the disaster-plan "cookbook."

Disaster trainings should never be boring! Mine never are. In fact, I have clients who specifically ask to be on shift during my live trainings because I make them immersive and interesting. I once turned down a big contract from a Silicon Valley company that didn't want to do in-person training at all. They wanted people to use an online system that simply parroted the basic lines in an emergency. They didn't believe in actual hands-on training and thought virtual tests would be enough. I'm telling you: it's not. In fact, when I ran anti-terrorism training for new EMTs with a book only, they made mistakes and didn't perform well in drills. So the next day I left the class textbook on the desk and had the EMTs simulate coming on scene and dealing with dozens of victims by placing mannequins throughout the room.

Have you noticed that people on the Food Network never make chopping celery seem boring? That's because it doesn't have to be, just like disaster trainings. Training families in an engaging way can be done easily. In fact, you can train them without them even realizing it. Pick a day when everyone is in a different area. Then text everyone to go to a certain restaurant at a certain time for dinner as a surprise.

The key here is to make sure that as many members of the family are physically separated as possible when you make the announcement. Then, at some point during the dinner, tell everyone that the restaurant will be the primary evacuation location in case of a disaster. It's an easy, nonthreatening way to train everyone on where the location is. Food is always a great motivator, and it also does something many disaster trainings fail to do—it provides a positive association with the disaster plan, making it easier for everyone to remember.

At your workplace, if you don't get trained, then train yourself. One easy training you can do for yourself is the basic evacuation drill. Here's what I want you to do: for one week, only take the stairs as you leave the building. *Especially* do this if you work in a tall skyscraper. And, if possible, take a different stairwell every time. It might take a while to reach the exit, but that's good because then you'll know the required time to leave, the route to take, and where the exit will place you if you're evacuating in an emergency.

This is a good exercise, even if your building is just a few floors high. I once visited a colleague in Southern California, and his office was on the fourth floor. We went out to lunch, and on the way back, I asked if we could take the stairs back up. As we ascended the stairs, he realized for the first time that the floor he was on needed a code for entry from the stairs. Obviously, he didn't know the code and had to call someone. What if there had been an incident during lunch and he couldn't get back into the office? Remember, you are responsible for your own disaster preparedness. Don't be a bystander.

Drills

The best way to Carry Out a drill is this: conduct it as if it is the real thing. Transform your drill into a *West Side Story* dress rehearsal. If you're running a fire drill, pretend a real fire is happening. Pick a room and imagine it's covered in flames. Have simulated victims. Create confusion. Simulate the chaos that would inevitably accompany any flash evacuation. Make sure the people who would normally be in charge are "injured."

I love drills. I go all out to the point where people love going through my drills because they empower them. I do that by forcing them to take responsibility for what is going on, assemble a team, and Carry Out the tasks successfully. When I do that, they instantly turn from bystanders to active disaster leaders. The key here is that the plan, the training, and the EST have to be in total sync with one another in empowering anyone to effectively lead.

Here's something I like to do: I'll pick a boss or a manager—or anyone else who would seem like a critical person for the disaster response to be successful—and I'll inform them that they'll have to sit on the sidelines and can't do anything for half of the drill.

Then I'll pick an employee in the back—usually the one who looks the most nervous. I'll casually inform them that they will be placed in charge. Throughout the drill, I'll walk them through the C3 Method, and at some point during the drill, their demeanor will change. They'll realize they can do this. I become their disaster-planning Rachael Ray.

Whatever institutions you are affiliated with, you should participate in at least one of their drills. If they don't have any, then create one yourself. For example, you should have your child's school conduct a dismissal as if evacuating the entire campus during a disaster. You might think this would be chaotic and confusing. I say . . . good! Better to address that now than when a real 8.0 earthquake strikes the school and we're still trying to remove the price tag on the generator. You should also know what every alert sounds like in your community. One of the biggest problems during the Three Mile Island nuclear disaster was that not a single person knew what the alerts from the complex were when the first sounds went off. This sparked panic and confusion, and people had no idea how to react appropriately. Thankfully, that disaster changed many policies in this regard. When I used to go surfing as a teenager, test alerts from the nuclear reactor in San Onofre would sometimes go off. The first time, it freaked me out, but after a while, I knew exactly what that sound was. Make sure you are aware of all the alerts in your workplace, school, or home.

A large concern in disaster after disaster is that organizations and people have no idea how first responders will handle an emergency. The solution to this is to run a disaster drill with actual first responders, even if that means a serious inconvenience. They do take time and resources, but they can make a major difference.

My favorite episode of the television series *Parks and Recreation* is when the state emergency manager arrives at the office during a day when the parks-and-rec department is extremely busy organizing a big celebration. When he arrives to inform them of the drill, the manager introduces himself in a deadpan, monotone voice: "I'm head of the Indiana Department of Emergency Preparedness, and today, I'm going to bring death and destruction to your town."

Amy Poehler's character Leslie is crestfallen about the timing, but, trying to be confident, says, "We're more than prepared for your test, but . . . um . . . it just so happens that today is a little inconvenient."

Without missing a beat, the emergency manager responds gleefully, "Good, because the best day for a drill is when it's inconvenient for everyone."[27]

I laugh every time I watch that scene because while government agencies don't do that in real life (public-sector drills are scheduled months and sometimes even years in advance), that emergency manager is living out *my dream*: the ultimate unscheduled disaster drill. The reason I like it so much is because disasters don't come on schedule and never come at a convenient time. If they did, we wouldn't call them disasters. We would call them "the days I stayed home from work."

Not only do scheduled drills inaccurately reflect the realities of a real disaster, but they also create a false sense of security, disempower students or employees, and reinforce the idea that the principal, administration, or supervisors will be in charge while the rest of us can just sit back and do nothing. Furthermore, no one learns anything from such drills.

When I get hired to do scheduled drills with schools, I test the weaknesses of their disaster plans with the C3 Method. Here's something that could work for you, too: I have a dreaded drill I invented, the "Baptism of Fire," where I'll give each teacher a sealed envelope with a sheet of paper inside. Each sheet of paper will have various complications that make running the drill much more difficult. For example, it might say something like, "You've been injured, so you must stay where you are." We might have one that says, "If you're a teacher, hide so that no one can find you." Another one might say, "Refuse to leave your classroom under any circumstances and refuse to allow your students to leave the classroom for any reason." I'll then mess with the EST, like switching the padlocks on the storage units so that people will have to figure out which key goes in which lock. You would be amazed at how long it can take to fix this common issue.

I'll then start the fire drill. How do you think it goes? It gets *West Side Story*–chaotic in a hurry. If I'm really feeling sadistic that day, I'll force them to do more difficult things, like have the principal stay in the office and not do anything. Or I'll take the most critical person, the one the disaster plan says is the *one* person who has to be involved, and I'll tell them that they were injured in the disaster. I'll have them lie down in their office and yell the f-word any time anyone tries to move them or come near them because they're in so much pain. (I can tell you that in my time, I've heard some Academy Award–caliber performances.)

In companies, I try to do the same thing: I'll identify critical managers or personnel and make sure they sit on the sidelines during the drill. In fact, I usually don't even allow them in the same room as the participants so that employees can have complete freedom of action without being under the eyes of a supervisor or able to look over to their bosses for guidance. I also require all employees to leave behind their name badges, and one really fun thing I like to do is actually take their organization chart and intentionally flip it upside down so that the line employees are running the drill while senior management is told to follow all instructions given to them. I don't do this torture exercise because

I enjoy seeing senior managers squirm (well, maybe a little); I do it because I want to see how effectively the plan empowers line employees and how well they have been trained to act in an emergency. When I run a drill of this type, it becomes instantly clear where the problems lie.

I'm not expecting you to run a full disaster drill in your home. I'm not naïve. But there are other ways you can gain drill experience. For instance, school drills are terrific ways to get kids involved and give them something that builds teamwork, creates confidence, and familiarizes them with disaster procedures in an engaging environment. When hired by a PTA or school, I usually take over the multipurpose room or an unused classroom, group kids from different classes and grades who don't know each other, and then have them run through a basic disaster scenario, giving the kids lots of authority and providing them with a realistic set of activities to perform, like setting up disaster equipment or preparing an area for first responders. I will also sometimes include a teacher or staff member who is not associated with any of the kids and then run through a simulated disaster together using the actual school disaster plan. Everyone has a great time; students get to meet and develop camaraderie with kids and teachers they might never otherwise interact with, and the drill gives them real skills they can use if a disaster strikes the school. I'll do these in thirty-minute intervals and run multiple sessions at the same time. The kids always get a lot out of it and have fun, which gives them a positive association with disaster response. By doing this, I give them a lesson they never forget, and it makes them excited about participating in a disaster response that actually empowers them.

Getting people excited about your disaster plan is what true disaster planning is all about. If you are at home, incorporate the whole family. At your child's school, encourage them to put on a fun drill like I just described. At work, get your employees actively involved. Sometimes I do get pushback when employers tell me that they would never trust their employees to do anything in a disaster response. But what I say to them is: Why did you hire them in the first place? Why do they work for you? Because in disasters, you are going to need them, and they are going to need you.

Lessons from Drills

If you are a member of an organization with an established disaster plan, hold a quick meeting after a drill and ask everyone to tell you what went well and what needs to be improved. In emergency management, we call this a "hotwash." It is essentially a way to capture the lessons from the drill on paper while they are still fresh in everyone's mind. We can then incorporate these lessons into the disaster plan. A hotwash document can make all the difference when determining how a disaster program is performing. Create a report, then implement the lessons in an improvement plan. This doesn't have to be hard or complicated. In fact, when I run my post-drill meetings, they're often a chance for people to have a good laugh at what happened during the drill, which not only teaches them some good lessons in a nonthreatening atmosphere but also positively reinforces the disaster program as a whole.

When you run drills correctly, you will be empowered and no longer reliant on someone else to take care of you in a real disaster. You will have run through realistic scenarios where many people are working together as a real team, and you will know how to Carry Out an effective response to a real disaster. This will make you less dependent on other agencies and people and will place the control where it should always be: on you.

WRAPPING UP: DRILLS CAN'T RUN ON FUMES

Training and drills are a critical part of your disaster-preparedness program. They provide you with invaluable tools that you can use to prepare for and during any disaster. However, your drills must get away from Shakespeare and mimic *West Side Story*'s chaos and action. This is the only way you can accurately replicate the experience of a real incident. Use the C3 Method to execute and apply drills correctly—your programs will benefit immensely as a result.

At the school I mentioned in the beginning of this chapter, I eventually convinced the staff to get the generator started. They located the manual and were trying to find the switch to turn it on when they realized that the generator had no gas in it. After some conversation, one of the teachers, exasperated, ran to his car so he could drive to the gas station, get some gas for the generator, and return to fill it up, while the rest of the drill came to a halt.

After about twenty minutes, he returned with two completely full gas cans. Lugging one of them, he and two other people set the generator outside the storage pod and prepared to finally fill it up. As they removed the gas caps to fill the generator, however, the custodian, more than a little curious, asked him what kind of gas he had purchased. "Eighty-seven, of course," he replied. Upon hearing this, the custodian quickly put his hand over the caps to prevent anyone from inserting the gas. This caused more than a little frustration until he had the unfortunate duty of informing them: this was a diesel generator.

Chapter Five

THE GASP: DON'T BE CALM. BE FOCUSED.

I once ran an active-shooter drill at very large and skilled nursing facility on the East Coast. I decided to run it in one part of the building, but had to use the building-wide PA system to make announcements regarding the drill. I selected an employee of the facility to make the announcements and showed her the script she would be using.

I carefully went over her lines with her, emphasizing that she must start and end every announcement with: "This is a drill; this is a drill." Everything went fine until she had to announce that there was an active shooter in the hallway. At that point, she was to say, "This is a drill; this is a drill. There is an active shooter in the hallway. Code Red lockdown. This is a drill; this is a drill." Instead, she took two deep breaths and, ignoring the script entirely, yelled into the PA system: "THERE'S A MAN WITH A GUN IN THE BUILDING!"

The pandemonium that ensued is difficult to describe in rational terms. But, as you can imagine, I had a bit of a problem on my hands. Guests ran from the hallways, social workers took cover, and you never saw eighty-year-old ladies wheel themselves that fast into their rooms. I immediately tried to undo the damage with a second announcement, but it was too late. Panic had set in, and it would take a herculean effort to reverse it. All the drill participants, as shocked as the residents, looked to me as to what they should do next. I turned to them and said, "Well, it's as close to real as we're going to get. Let's go." And they immediately got to work.

It is those first moments that set the tone for any disaster response—because that's when you have to make the internal decision to be a leader or a bystander.

In part one of this book, you learned how to create an effective disaster-preparedness program, from writing and evaluating a basic disaster plan that actually empowers you to purchasing equipment, supplies, and technology that serve you instead of making you fully dependent on them. Then I walked you away from the "Shakespearean drills" and showed you how to turn them into dynamic *West Side Story* rehearsals.

Welcome to opening night. Disaster strikes, and the curtain goes up.

This initial moment is what I term the "Gasp" because that's the instinctual reaction that occurs when you realize a disaster is occurring. Depending on the situation and the suddenness of it, your physiological reaction will vary, but no matter what, that initial Gasp—and how you deal with it—will have a major impact on the rest of the disaster response. If you have ever participated in high school or amateur theater, you know that when the curtain goes up on that first night, there is indeed a Gasp.

Even disasters you have been through before will create a certain amount of stress, whether anticipated or not. The issue isn't having nerves in the moment after a disaster strikes—you're going to have them. The Gasp, as I call it, is normal. The question is: What will you do with those nerves?

YOU PANIC IN A DISASTER

The first major problem is when you panic in a disaster. Panic is a serious problem in disaster management. When in the presence of danger, the normal physiological response is one of three options: fight, flight, or freeze.[28] Each of these is impulsive and can cause people to do unsafe, counterproductive, or just generally unwise things.

Let's define each of these reactions. When someone decides to **fight**, they decide to face the danger head-on. A good example of the fight response is when someone is attacking you with a weapon and you attempt to wrestle it out of

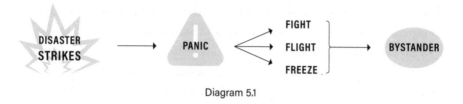

Diagram 5.1

their hands. When you are in **flight** mode, it means you are running away from the threat to get as far away from it as possible. If you watch any alien-invasion movie or big-budget disaster film, you'll get a pretty good idea of what this looks like in practice. Last is the **freeze** response. When you freeze, your body goes into a state of serious inaction. This is common when someone is mugged or faced with a life-threatening staredown with a dangerous animal.

The physiology of these responses is well documented, and, while everyone is a little different, you will likely experience a combination of the following during a Gasp:

- **Heart rate:** Your heart beats faster to bring oxygen to your major muscles. In a freeze response, your heart rate can increase or decrease.
- **Lungs:** Your breathing speeds up to deliver more oxygen to your blood. In a freeze response, you might hold your breath or restrict breathing.
- **Eyes:** Your peripheral vision increases to help you notice your surroundings. Your pupils dilate and let in more light, which helps you see better.
- **Ears:** Your ears "perk up," and your hearing becomes sharper.
- **Blood:** Blood thickens, which increases clotting factors. This prepares your body for injury.
- **Skin:** Your skin might produce more sweat or get cold. You may look pale or have goosebumps.
- **Hands and feet:** As blood flow increases to your major muscles, your hands and feet might get cold.
- **Pain perception:** The fight and flight responses temporarily reduce your perception of pain.

When you review these, you might notice something: they all put your body's functions at a heightened state of awareness. This is really important—in a disaster, that's exactly what you want. Go back and reread the list, thinking about how each one of those symptoms could provide you a tremendous advantage in responding to an emergency. So many people, however, try to battle and suppress these symptoms, but that actually makes them more powerless.

The word "panic" originates from the Greek god Pan, who in ancient Greek mythology is depicted as half man, half goat, and likes to play the pipes. There are many stories about his merrymaking skills, but he also loved his afternoon naps, which he would take in local caves. And when anyone woke him, he would let out a terrifying scream. When Hellenistic Greeks would hear any frightening sounds, they would blame it on *panikon deima*, or "panic fear."[29]

Panikon deima is exactly what happens when no one takes Command. The moment when disaster occurs, most people start fleeing for their lives. We see this all the time in the movies and in real life. The more powerless people become, the more chaos ensues, the more people are unempowered and become victims, and the more the problem compounds. This then creates an unending saga of issues. Regardless of which of three responses one lands in after disaster strikes—fight, flight, or freeze—this creates an everyone-for-themselves scenario that will result in complete paralysis. Perhaps the saddest case of this came from the famous Triangle Shirtwaist Factory fire that occurred on March 25, 1911. The fire caused the deaths of over one hundred people, most of whom were immigrant women. The panic that ensued when the fire started caused the elevator to become overloaded with people, as the fire doors were locked by management and there were no alternate means of escape. This led to even greater fear amid the anxious people trying to get out, which further increased the panic.

I've actually seen many medical emergencies where someone will randomly collapse, and the people around them will run away, acting like a grenade just dropped. They will literally start running in different directions. I used to be an event EMT working at large event venues. One day, I worked at a semiprofessional hockey game, and a spectator got hit in the face with a puck that had flown from the ice. He was bleeding profusely and clearly in much pain. As I was descended the stairs to reach him, however, I noticed that people were running the other way, up the stairs past me. In fact, I had difficulty pushing through the crowd to get to the man.

A few people wanted to help and tried to talk to and reassure him, but everyone else looked completely freaked out. People tend to panic when they aren't really sure what to do. And relying on instinct instead of training will not give you the best information to use in your emergency response. When everyone acts from a place of instinct rather than preparedness, confusion spreads throughout the scene. You won't slow down and assess the scene. Then, because of the confusion, more panic will spread, creating further confusion. This will become a never-ending cycle because your mindset will stay paralyzed.

The way people fight this impulse to panic is by trying to stay artificially calm. However, you're not going to be calm in a disaster, so why try to fake it? I can't stand it when plans and training try to instill in people a sense that they should stay calm in a disaster. It's tremendously destructive and unhelpful. What does "calm" mean? The definition is to not show or feel nervousness, anger, or other strong emotions. Why? That won't help you. In a disaster, being calm means being in a state of passivity. In a disaster, this creates a dangerous situation—your forced calmness will just make you more nervous and will increase the agitation levels around you. Paralysis will occur.

If people stay calm during a disaster, it means they're fighting their own mindset, which puts them at a mental disadvantage. When you try to stay calm, you're actually relying on someone else to handle the problem while you remain in a passive, inactive state.

In such scenarios, no one takes charge in the moments after a disaster. Everyone turns into a bystander. Sometimes it's because they're frozen in fear; other times, they don't want to act and risk being sued; still other times, they might be afraid of being ridiculed for responding in a certain way. In an organizational setting, if no one is in charge, the Communication will become jumbled and confused, and problems will compound into bigger ones. It becomes every person for themself.

Fortunately, you can learn to navigate the Gasp by using the C3 Method.

C3 METHOD SOLUTIONS

Leadership and responsibility make all the difference when it comes to turning the energy within a Gasp into a valuable tool rather than your greatest weakness. You can acquire both through the C3 Method.

COMMAND – "I CAN EMPOWER MYSELF"

Taking Command allows you to set the stage for taking responsibility for what happens to you in a disaster and leads to personal empowerment. This is *your* disaster, and you're going to navigate it successfully. This is not the time for debate or discussion. *You must take Command of yourself first.* The best way to do this is to use the energy around you to immediately focus on what is happening.

In a disaster, as I've explained, being calm is unhelpful because it causes you to fight against valuable energy that you could be redirecting into your disaster response. I don't want you to do that. I want you to take that energy and harness it so that it becomes your greatest strength in the moments after a disaster strikes.

The Japanese martial art of aikido is translated as "way of harmonizing energy." It's a unique martial art because it relies almost exclusively on using the energy your opponent expends against them. Instead of emphasizing kicks and punches, it focuses on grips, throws, and locks. Those who practice aikido believe that their own energy shouldn't be wasted trying to stop someone else's. It should be maximized by converting the opponent's energy against themself.

This is how I want you to use your "life energy" to design any disaster. This is how you will take your response from a place of false positivity to an active design state. A place where you now assert your own control over your own disaster. A place where you must take yourself from a panicked posture to a focused posture in the moments after a disaster strikes.

In a disaster, of course you are going to be nervous. You are going to be in a state of hyperactivity, and the adrenaline is going to be pumping. That's great. That's what you should want. The key is to take that energy and use it to your advantage. That's why nature gave you that response. It is there to protect you and can be an incredible asset in a disaster. Don't squander it by trying to remain calm. Why would you want to remain calm when the energy of those nerves can give you a competitive edge against the chaos of a disaster?

Don't be calm. Ever. Like in aikido, I want you to redirect your energy to your advantage through focus. Focus involves putting all your attention into one action. What it does is concentrate an action into motion. I want you to stop trying to be calm. When you're calm, you're in a place of passivity. *I don't want you to be calm. I want you to be focused.* Because if you don't focus, there will be chaos.

If the word "calm" is in your disaster plans, please remove it. Don't ever direct people to be calm. It's unrealistic and silly. I mean, do you really expect people to be calm when someone is shooting an AK-47 in the hallways? I see this all the time—someone writes an active-shooter plan, and during training they say, "Well, first thing I want you to do is remain calm." If I wanted calm, I would listen to a jazz station on late-night radio. Remain ready. Remain focused.

At my company, we use dark-blue or black backpacks in emergency-response situations, but *never* red. My company is probably the only one in the world doing this, but we do it because blue signifies focus and stability. Red is a chaos sign and increases negative anxiety. I want people focused during times of stress, and even this minor change can have major results.

This is the reason I hate it when people call their disaster backpack a "bug-out bag." I was introduced to this term during a presentation I delivered a number of years ago. It has grated on me ever since. The reason I hate it is because it implies that you have lost all mental sense by the time you use the backpack and that its contents are instruments of your insanity.

Of course there will be nervous energy and a feeling of being overwhelmed in the beginning. Redirect it. If you can focus by using the C3 Method, starting with gaining Command over yourself, you can redirect this energy rather than fight it and respond to a disaster quickly and effectively. This step is incredibly valuable and will give you the personal-management tools to put yourself on the right footing in an emergency and move you from a *panicked* posture to a *focused* one.

COMMUNICATE - "I CAN EMPOWER OTHERS"

Once you have gained Command of yourself, your next obligation is to get others out of their panic and into a focused posture, too. Depending on the disaster, this may or may not be instantaneous. Literally ask yourself, "What's going on here?" Then go below the surface. If safety is an issue, don't fool around. Get to safety immediately. Afterward, do whatever you have to do to get the people around you out of their fight, flight, or freeze responses. Get people into the focused posture that will empower them to start acting rationally.

This isn't just relevant to the obvious emergency situations where immediate action is clearly necessary, like a fire or a flood. I'm also talking about those disasters that may not be immediately apparent to those in an office, like a rabid wild animal doing its Cujo impression on the ground floor of the building or a natural gas leak in the parking lot outside. Effectively Communicating these circumstances is critical to ensuring that all employees are in a heightened state of awareness and able to move into a more focused state. Here is a good example of what this team formulation will look like.

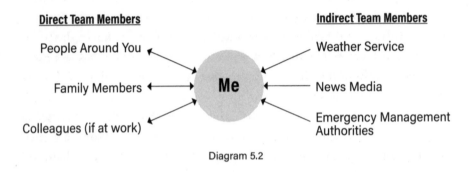

Diagram 5.2

You will notice that everyone around you is a direct team member. (As a reminder, *indirect* team members include news organizations and PA-system announcements in a subway or building.) One thing that will happen after you take Command and get people out of a panicked state is that you will start sorting out who will really stay and be a part of the disaster response and who won't. That doesn't make the ones who leave cowards; they might just have other priorities. Don't fight this. For example, during the BP oil spill in 2010, I oversaw the emergency program for twenty-three dock sites spread across four states. I created emergency cards for the dock supervisors. On the back of the cards, I wrote, "Take care of yourself and your family first! Once they are safe, come to work." I also write this on the back of my business card, which can double as an emergency card.

At schools, this is critically important, as some people will, upon hearing about a disaster, run to the school to try to grab their kids during a disaster. This can be problematic for schools that are trying to sort out who is allowed to take which child and need to make sure that every student is accounted for in the initial evacuation.

After you have taken Command and established the right information to Communicate, your next obligation is to help everyone get Command of themselves. Safety is imperative. Keep people moving. Get everyone out of their inaction and panic. The way to get things done is by *signaling the start of the disaster response.* This could even be a text message to your family or some other technological communication, but regardless of the method, you must signify that the disaster response is beginning. At Disneyland, the crowd snapped out of its inaction after I clapped my hands.

A clap or other loud sound, like a whistle, can be a great in-person technique. It tends to get people's attention. My late grandfather was in the Navy during World War II, and he was stationed on large ships in the South Pacific. He had this loud whistle that he'd perfected because many of his shipmates could not hear him when he was trying to get their attention. This skill became of great use to him when he was a high school teacher later in life to get kids out of their inaction right away. That's what I want you to do. Find an action that can break through the noise and get people focused. It needs to be assertive, it needs to be out loud, and it needs to be unusual. Don't be calm and reactive—that doesn't empower anyone. You must break through that initial hesitation in the Gasp that turns people into bystanders. You are making this disaster *your* incident. And when you signal the start of the disaster response, you will prompt the sifting process of bystander versus responder. The latter group will form your team.

Each person in your team is now critical and an empowered participant. Next, Communicate so that emergency services can be activated right away. Calling 911 is usually a good start, but depending on the disaster, you may also need to reach out to suicide or mental-health crisis hotlines or other services.

Once you've gotten focused and redirected others, you have one job. Just one. Figure out what's going on. That's all! Don't try to do anything else until you really know what's going on. This can be a quick process—if you see a tanker truck overturn, followed by a sudden explosion and plume of green gas, it might seem obvious what's going on.

But is it? Things aren't always what they seem. I once wrote a disaster plan for a church that worked entirely remotely. All of its services were conducted online through live and recorded video. One day, the church faced a cyberattack that seemed at first like an innocuous single email-phishing scam. The offending email was deleted, and the incident was forgotten. However, about a week later, the church's website was the subject of a denial-of-service attack. What the church leaders hadn't realized was that just opening the email had given the hacker the ability to embed malicious code on the church's server. It took a significant amount of time and money for the church to regain control of it.

If you're showing up to an emergency already in progress, don't be shy. Ask someone what's going on. Look around for clues that will give you an indication of not only what the disaster is but also what the hazards are. By staying quiet, you remain in a passive, bystander state.

But don't overplay the incident, either. Focus on what has happened, and don't catastrophize. Overreaching can be just as bad as underreacting because it can spread chaos and confusion, which inevitably leads to panic. Keeping your mindset in a focused perspective instead of trying to artificially stay calm will direct your energies in a positive way.

CARRY OUT - "WE CAN EMPOWER EACH OTHER"

Finally, you can start working with your team to address the situation. Be aware that as you figure out what's going on and get others out of their inattention and into a state of hypervigilance, some will leave. That's okay. People must decide for themselves. If they don't want to be part of the team, let them go. Forget about them.

Again, this doesn't mean you are going to be permanently taking over the disaster scene. It means that you are asserting immediate control to get things started so that others can later come help. But don't put yourself in a bystander state and let the scene run itself—this will make you vulnerable.

WRAPPING UP: BE ANYTHING OTHER THAN CALM

Assessing the scene is arguably the most important step in any incident response. It provides the basic information you need to respond effectively. All subsequent actions are going to be completely dependent on what you learn in the first moments after you realize a disaster has struck. Assessing effectively and focusing yourself and your energy through the C3 Method will sustain you through the rest of the disaster. The key is to not fight your immediate emotions but to instead redirect them, similar to the techniques of aikido. Your instinctive reactions, when properly refocused, can be transformed from your greatest weakness to your greatest strength and allow you to design any disaster.

After the blown active-shooter drill at the skilled nursing facility, I was eventually able to assure everyone and return things to normalcy. While I was completing the after-action report, I decided to review the facility's disaster plan to see where I could improve it based on the drill. I made some modifications to the lockdown procedures and even made a small change to where the disaster plans would be kept.

I will never forget the last line of the plan, which I read as I neared the end of my review: "Be calm."

Chapter Six

IS THE SCENE SAFE?

S everal years ago, I ran an earthquake drill at a small resort in Yosemite, California. I decided that for this drill I would add an additional complication for the participants: a dog. I borrowed a very well-behaved dog named Ranger from one of the nonparticipating employees and placed him strategically on the second floor of the clubhouse where we would run the drill. I didn't tell any of the participants the dog was there. During the pre-drill briefing, I told participants that they would have to evacuate the entire building of every person or pet. The disaster we were simulating was a major earthquake, so there would likely be injuries and hazards all over the building—and they had just twenty-five minutes to get everyone evacuated.

I signaled the start of the drill, and everyone began their usual scurrying around. When the rescuers got to the second floor, they noticed the dog, just panting and looking like he wanted to be petted. I had placed a sign next to him: "You MUST evacuate this dog." However, what they didn't notice was the pile of wires I had scattered on the ground in front of Ranger, paired with a piece of paper labeling it as "Live Wires." Responder after responder tried to touch the dog, and once they did so, one of my drill supervisors would touch the responder and say, "You're electrocuted. Play dead." And one by one, about five responders went through this process until there was a large pile of them in front of the dog.

After the drill, when I spoke to each of the "victims" who fell for the ruse, they told me the same thing: they couldn't leave the dog behind. They told me that even if the sign hadn't been there instructing them to evacuate the dog, they would have tried to anyway.

I did this intentionally to teach them a valuable lesson about disaster response: they must protect themselves first. Of course, I wanted them to evacuate the dog; that's why I wrote the sign. But they had to learn how to do it safely. They had to learn the hard way that ensuring safety on the scene is critical for any responder. Once you have assessed the scene, your life becomes the most important priority in your initial disaster response. You must take care of yourself, and you can properly do that using the C3 Method.

Disaster scenes can be very dangerous. In chapter five, I talked about getting out of your immediate shock and moving from a panicked posture to a focused one. The second thing I want you to do is protect yourself.

Problems surface when people assume a disaster scene is safe before they act. This creates serious issues of safety and health that are too often disregarded in the moment.

YOU PERFORM DANGEROUS ACTIONS

In almost every major disaster, people routinely enter scenes that are unsafe. In 2005, for example, according to an estimate by the Centers for Disease Control and Prevention, between September 12 and October 11, a total of 27,135 patient visits for injury or illness were reported by response workers in the aftermath of Hurricane Katrina.[30] In Houston, evacuees from the Gulf Coast also overwhelmed local health clinics with injuries and illnesses associated with the hurricane. This kind of situation creates a compounding problem for not only emergency management but also first responders who are working the scene because they now have additional injuries to handle with resources that are already stretched to their limits. Many of these types of injuries can easily be prevented by people properly assessing the scene. We notice a hazard like broken glass or major floodwaters, and we go forward anyway, thinking that it won't injure us. But by doing that, we surrender control of the disaster to a dangerous, unpredictable scene.

YOU DON'T GAIN PROPER KNOWLEDGE OF THE HAZARD

It's human nature to believe you can handle things on your own. But I'm telling you . . . you can't. So don't try. Hurricane Katrina is a notable example where there were hidden hazards that even the experienced New Orleanians were not expecting. Bacteria in water, electrical lines, wild animals, and armed criminals were just a few of the hazards that resulted from the 134-miles-per-hour winds of the storm and the subsequent flooding after the levees failed.[31]

Often, there will be hazards that you have not considered. For instance, it's very common to discover a bomb after an active-shooter incident. During the April 1999 Columbine shootings, the two young men placed ninety-nine bombs around the school, which were actually propane tanks that had been tied together in a rudimentary fashion.[32] One of the things that witnesses later discussed was how they'd seen the young men shooting but couldn't figure out what they were shooting at.

They weren't shooting at the evacuating victims. They were shooting at the propane tanks around the school. They were hoping to detonate one or two of them, which would then create a chain reaction of explosions, compromising the building and resulting in a collapse of the structure. They had intended to blow up the school.

Even before a disaster strikes, an area can be completely unsafe. For months leading up to the Oroville Dam crisis in 2017, the entire community of Oroville in the Sacramento Valley was unsafe. El Niño rains had caused Lake Oroville to nearly top the spillway of the dam. Authorities, against the advice of experts, warned that the bedrock wouldn't hold up and would unleash millions of gallons of water into the community. While the emergency was addressed and no collapse occurred, over 180,000 people evacuated the area in fear of severe flooding.

Some hazards can't be seen even if you are looking for them. Radiation, for example, is invisible, odorless, and tasteless (not that you would want to taste it), and it can cause acute or chronic illness (such as cancer) and even death. Other particulate matter in old buildings may contain asbestos that can suddenly release into the air. During 9/11, for example, these particulates resulted in the death of thousands of people from cancer years afterward, including a Sacramento FBI agent.[33]

There are also hazards that can inflict invisible wounds. For instance, psychological trauma and acute mental-illness symptoms can be invisible killers. Witnessing traumatic incidents and walking into unstable areas can cause psychological scars that may never heal. Every year, there are hundreds of first responders who commit suicide. After a major disaster, that number usually doubles. There's also "survivor's guilt," when a person feels guilty because they survived a life-threatening event that others did not.[34] This is typically associated with PTSD and can initially show up as acute stress disorder and result in a series of other psychological difficulties that may not manifest right away.[35]

While there is no way of completely preventing disaster trauma, there is a way to exacerbate it: walking into scenes totally unprepared for them.

YOU DON'T FULLY RESPECT THE HAZARD

Many people think they can control a hazard by "being careful." Normally, this is an issue that comes from being particularly familiar with a certain hazard or area. One example is when people drive through floodwaters, even though there is *no instance* when this is safe. This is such a significant problem that the US National Weather Service has a program called "Turn Around Don't Drown" that highlights flood-driving safety. Yet, every year, many people are still killed by driving through floodwaters. Some survivors of this experience told officials that they felt they would be safe as long as they were "careful." What they don't realize, however, is that there are indicators of unsafe floodwaters that cannot be assessed by drivers.

But I think the most prevalent example of this is when people try to rescue animals. Many well-meaning people try to rescue animals because they assume they need a place to go and are loathe to leave them on the side of the road. As a pet parent, I 100 percent understand this feeling. However, to say this is a reckless and dangerous activity is putting it mildly. What many people don't seem to realize is that any animal can revert to its natural state when severely stressed and can act violently as a result. Dog owners of various types who think they know how to handle dogs are often bitten during major disaster responses—this goes for both strays and animals you already know. Pet bites and severe scratches are extremely common. Many times, owners have never seen their animals in a stressed state and therefore don't know the indicators beforehand.

Other safety issues abound in a disaster. I worked in Louisiana for many years and was living in Baton Rouge when Hurricane Gustav made landfall in September. Within a week, I was reading reports of people who had put their generators in their homes and started them, resulting in carbon-monoxide poisoning cases, a few of which led to fatalities. Even years later, I never fail to hear about families who take a diesel generator, place it in the middle of their living space, and rev it up.

YOU FOCUS ON SOMETHING ELSE

Distracted focus is perhaps the reason why most disaster injuries occur. Like with the dog near the "Live Wires" during the disaster drill, people tend to focus on one thing that distracts them from the safety of the scene, even to their own detriment. For instance, the first two steps in CPR have nothing to do with the victim you are trying to help.[36] They are meant to protect you as a rescuer. Step one is assessing the scene around you for safety, which is a derivative of what I told you about in chapter five. The second step in CPR after assessing the scene is putting on body substance isolation, also known as personal protective equipment (PPE). Years ago, when I would write about PPE in many of my disaster plans, few people had any idea what I was talking about. Today, in the wake of the COVID-19 pandemic, everyone knows what PPE means.

When I train brand-new EMTs on how to respond to a hazardous-materials incident, I simulate a chemical spill in a parking lot by taking a bright yellow barrel with hazardous materials markings, filling it halfway with water, and tossing dry ice inside to make it look like gas is escaping—and then I tip the barrel over. Then I place some actors who behave as victims nearby.

When the EMTs arrive in the ambulance, I have the actors call out to them to help. Inevitably, some of the EMT trainees will jump out of the ambulance by instinct and run with their gear to help without first assessing the scene and getting themselves properly suited up to enter the scene. I'll immediately inform them that they are now victims of the chemical spill themselves and will tell them to lie down and wait for assistance. I do this because I am trying to train them to *take their focus away from the victims and to focus on the scene itself.*

Other simulations I have done include child actors in a bus who start yelling at EMTs to help them. The EMTs will try to drag victims out of the bus, getting covered in the "chemical" and inadvertently contaminating the children at the same time.

By not taking scene safety seriously, you are putting yourself in serious physical and psychological jeopardy. This is not only a tragedy by itself; it also compounds the problems on scene.

First, if you get injured or killed, you're taking resources away from others who need help because you will now be the focus of your attention. For example, the very last person to die in the 1995 Oklahoma City bombing was a nurse who worked at one of the local healthcare facilities. She heard the explosion and ran to the scene to help without bothering to talk to person in Command of the incident. She was later struck on the head by a computer monitor hanging from the fourth floor. Second, if you're injured, you can't help anybody else on scene. You are a valuable resource in a disaster, and you must be as protected as possible when a disaster strikes. This is especially true if you are a parent, a caregiver, or in a profession where you are taking care of a vulnerable person, such as at a nursing home. If you get injured, you can't help the very people that you're tasked with helping. Also, rescuers who can't find you will risk their lives to open every door and check every room, exposing themselves to extreme hazards in what is often a highly dangerous post-disaster environment. **That means someone else's son, daughter, husband, wife, brother, or sister is now risking their life to take care of you.** If a first-responder is injured or killed while trying to save you from something unwise or unsafe, how will you feel? Will you be able to live with that?

If, for example, you've ever flown in a modern commercial aircraft, you know about the obligatory safety presentation before takeoff where they tell you to put your mask on before helping anyone else. This is a Federal Aviation Administration regulation.[37] They don't have this rule because they hate kids. It's because they know that if there is a decompression in the cabin, you could be immediately incapacitated, and then you wouldn't be able to put a mask on your child. And even if you can get your child's mask on first, they might not be able to put a mask on you.

C3 METHOD SOLUTIONS

Keeping yourself safe during a disaster is a critical part of your response and requires a systematic approach and thought process. Ultimately, it's up to you. First responders, elected officials, and others can advise you, but you are in the end responsible for what happens to you and will have to accept the consequences of your actions.

COMMAND – "I CAN EMPOWER MYSELF"

This is one assumption I want you to make of every disaster scene, no matter what: *assume that the scene will kill you until you can prove otherwise.* Notice that I didn't say "injure." I said "kill." When I was a hazmat technician, I was trained on a concept called IDLH, which stands for "Immediately Dangerous to Life or Health." It's an acronym that was developed by the National Institute for Occupational Safety and Health to ensure that workers in contaminated work environments have both a high level of mask protection and the ability to escape in extreme emergencies.[38]

The reason I want you to use a high threshold for disaster response is because any disaster area is potentially IDLH for you. In addition, this assumption is critical to a successful execution of any disaster response because it naturally shifts the presumption of "If I do nothing, someone else will take care of it" to "If I do nothing, no one else will, either." You are telling yourself that no one can make sure you are safe but *you*—not the fire department, not FEMA, not law enforcement, not anyone else. That doesn't mean those organizations won't play a critical role in advising you—because they will. However, in the end, you are responsible for keeping yourself safe and not doing anything that will compound the disaster or complicate an already chaotic and emotional scene. This places you in an active, focused mindset over the passive, "calm" one where you are making dangerous assumptions about what might seem safe without taking in all the factors present. When you don't properly assess the scene and protect yourself, you put yourself at the mercy of the incidents around you. I want you to never take a scene for granted again.

You don't know what ultimate hazards might be present on scene, but armed the right mindset, you can put yourself in the best position to respond safely to a disaster. Let's talk about this in more detail.

There is no doubt that disaster scenes are unpredictable and hold many hidden hazards, which is why you should first assume that every disaster scene will kill you until you can prove otherwise. If you can't prove that a scene is safe, then it's dangerous to you, and you should immediately leave. That means you shouldn't try to ford that river with your car. That means you shouldn't run to the scene of an accident on the freeway unless you know that you are safe from whatever caused that accident, as well as the other hazards naturally associated with being on a busy freeway. Does that mean that after evaluating an incident, you'll be 100 percent safe? No, but it will give you the pause you need to prove its safety before doing so.

It's crucial to have the proactive mindset that you have to be constantly assessing the environment around you. If you automatically assume a scene is safe, you will let down your guard and become passive. But if you are always concerned about the safety of a scene, there is no way you will assume someone else will have taken care of things for you. You will reinforce that you must take responsibility for your own safety.

This can help keep you alert even in scenes with hidden hazards you haven't considered. Eric Robert Rudolph, also known as the Olympic Park Bomber, was actually a serial bomber. He was a member of a right-wing fanatical group and committed a series of terrorist attacks against abortion clinics in the early 1990s. In his bombings, he would set off a device and, after the explosion, would wait until first responders arrived. Once he saw them congregate in a certain place, he would detonate a secondary device, which would then maim or kill them.[39]

Never go off your "gut instinct" or say to yourself, "I've been in dozens of these, so I know what's safe." Because you don't. Treat every disaster exactly like what it is: a brand-new situation that you have never seen before. I grew up in Southern California and have experienced a number of earthquakes, both major and minor, and I can tell you that no two were exactly alike. In fact, not everyone realizes that there are four different kinds of earthquakes, each with its own unique associated hazards.

COMMUNICATE - "I CAN EMPOWER OTHERS"
Communication on these scenes is going to be critical. Since you must assume that the scene will kill you unless you can prove otherwise, it will be essential

for you to lean on first-response and other government agencies to assist you as you make critical decisions.

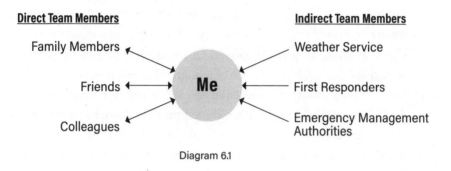

Direct Team Members   **Indirect Team Members**

Family Members   Weather Service

Friends   **Me**   First Responders

Colleagues   Emergency Management Authorities

Diagram 6.1

On your team, you may have a combination of direct and indirect members. First-response agencies and weather services will be powerful indirect team members because they can inform you on trends from previous injuries and likely safety hazards. But you should also speak to people around you—your direct team members—who may have already identified hazards nearby. You need to ask them; don't take them for granted. The people around you can be excellent and important team members in these situations.

Whatever sources you use, ensure that they are reliable. One of the ways that passive thinking sometimes creeps into early disaster-response discussions is when people rely on celebrities or social media rumors when making decisions. These are not reliable sources unless they have specialized knowledge or are accompanied by similar messages from emergency-management or first-response agencies.

Don't let a celebrity think for you; get firsthand information from agencies that know what they are doing, as they have an interest in providing you with correct information rather than a marketing statement. Accurate information is critical to making good decisions in a disaster. And remember that regardless of the information you receive, you must follow the assumption that if you can't prove the scene is safe, then some hazard can and will kill you.

CARRY OUT - "WE CAN EMPOWER EACH OTHER"

Now that you have your team, you must have a systematic approach to evaluating the conditions of your surroundings. When you are approaching a disaster scene, you should do so methodically so that you do not put anyone in a position of unnecessary danger. This process starts from the moment you determine the disaster has occurred.

Assess the Hazards

When you are going to perform an action, I want you to think beyond the disaster, just like in CPR or in EMS training. We don't arrive on scene and simply say, "They're hurt." We arrive and ask, "Why are they hurt?" or "What is the mechanism of injury?" or "What caused this?" Frankly, I only care about what the disaster is as long as it helps me look for possible threats. I don't want your focus on the disaster to pigeonhole you into thinking that a flood is "just a flood" or "just like ones I have seen a million times." This is not academic or splitting hairs—I have seen floodwaters that seem innocuous but are electrified. I have seen animals that in the previous five hurricanes were perfectly normal but in the sixth one, for some reason, are brought over the edge and end up biting their owners or others, even with a spotless history of docile behavior.

If a tornado touches down, I want you to think not about what happened (a destructive wind event) but about what the likely mechanisms of injury now are, like animals roaming the streets and other such mayhem (objects thrown everywhere, power lines down, cars overturned, etc.). That way, you can more accurately assess what is likely to harm you. This will also help you mentally get away from the word "tornado"—in the sense that you have been through them before—to a place where two-hundred-miles-per-hour winds cause dangers from electrical lines, animals, and countless other elements, naturally, and are therefore something new every time. Doing this will help you be more cognizant of the hazards that disasters inevitably create, as well as the secondary disasters they can spawn, like fires or gas explosions. With every one of these incidents, you must look more holistically at how it can harm you.

One of the misconceptions people have regarding hurricanes, for example, is that the wind is the most dangerous element of the storm. This is incorrect. It is the ensuing floods that are the most dangerous. Hurricanes also routinely spawn massive tornadoes. When you are assessing the hazards of a hurricane situation, then, you should anticipate and look ahead toward the destruction that floodwaters and tornadoes will cause. This way of thinking will give you an edge when you're faced with a disaster.

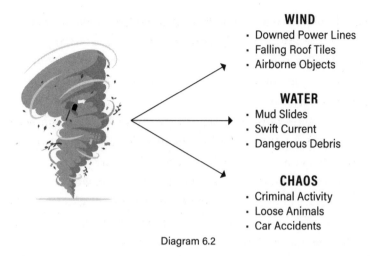

WIND
- Downed Power Lines
- Falling Roof Tiles
- Airborne Objects

WATER
- Mud Slides
- Swift Current
- Dangerous Debris

CHAOS
- Criminal Activity
- Loose Animals
- Car Accidents

Diagram 6.2

You can see in this diagram that I've taken a tornado and stripped it into its individual parts that could impact you: wind, water (from flash flooding), and chaos. (There are many more, but this is a good start.) Each of these parts is then tied to elements that could potentially kill you.

As you can see, the IDLH environment is multifaceted. Don't underestimate. Rely on Communication with first responders and others to tell you what is safe and what isn't, and remember to look past the surface level of an emergency. When a person is injured, for example, ask yourself: What made this person injured? Were they shot by an active assailant, attacked by a dog, or hit in the head from a falling roof tile? Each of these possibilities is a threat to you in its own way, and there can always be additional, hidden hazards—like radiation, chemicals, and bombs—that you won't easily see.

Avoid the Hazard

The best way to protect yourself against a hazard is to avoid it. So either prove that the scene is safe or leave. If you can't make the scene safe, back up, let first responders handle it, and then return later when it is safe. One way to do this is protect yourself first by wearing PPE at all times where appropriate. But you also must be aware of changing conditions, including safety hazards. In large natural disasters, look for electrical poles and unleashed or dangerous animals.

Avoiding a hazard means being self-aware as well. When I was a young EMT, I once worked at a scene for a long period of time without eating or drinking anything. At about hour twelve, I almost collapsed because I had forgotten to take care of myself. I could have easily avoided this hazard, either through scheduling, personal monitoring, or setting a personal alarm to eat and drink. However, when you are in the middle of a disaster and a lot is happening simultaneously, this can be difficult to do. When you are taking care of your family, don't forget about your own personal needs. If you aren't feeling well, take care of yourself right away; if you are incapacitated, then your family will be worse off as a result.

Avoiding the hazard puts you in the best position to protect yourself when you are faced with a disaster because there will be many instances where you can't reasonably remove the hazard or make it less dangerous. This is especially true for community-wide emergencies where there are multiple hazard areas or when a particularly destructive event creates life-threatening hazards across multiple buildings. The 2011 earthquake and tsunami in Japan is a good example of this.

Mitigate or Remove the Hazard

You can also mitigate or remove the hazard, which means making the hazard less effective. PPE is a good example of a mitigation technique. However, *if it is safe to do so*, rather than mitigate the hazard, you should attempt to remove it altogether.

However, there are easy ways to mitigate obvious hazards in a disaster. You can make sure that you are eating food and drinking water, for instance. During the BP oil spill, we had teams working in the Gulf of Mexico in July, when the humidity was at or near 100 percent. They wore cleanup suits and were sweating profusely to the point where their boots needed to be poured out after every entry to the scene. While there was nothing we could do about the heat, we made sure they were given fluids (including water and electrolytes) and long breaks between sessions to fight against dehydration. We also had spotters on every boat whose responsibility was to watch them and make sure that if any signs of heat-related illness (such as heat exhaustion or heat stroke) appeared, immediate medical intervention or evacuation to medical facilities onshore would be available.

Taking care of yourself from a psychological perspective is critical as well; seek help and support when you find yourself doing something you're not mentally prepared or able to do. In July 2021, a beloved North Carolina emergency-room physician died by suicide in her home just hours after a shift.[40] Throughout the COVID-19 pandemic, she had been working long, horrific shifts on the front lines. She had reached out to family and friends, who did their best to support her, but their support wasn't enough, and she eventually shot herself in her living room. This is not an isolated story. The acute psychological trauma from the pandemic and other associated disasters has created a serious, lingering public-health emergency with long-lasting effects.

There are psychological first-aid teams that are deployed throughout the country in response to major disasters. They work with disaster victims as well as responders. I lecture multiple times a year to graduate-level mental-health students around the United States, and the first thing I talk to them about is the effects on *themselves* when they deploy. The long-term effects of doing this kind of work are psychological and can leave lasting scars from being in unsafe scenes. What I tell them to do is use a buddy system where each one of them keeps one eye on another. That way, everyone will have someone watching them in case of distress.

WRAPPING UP: SAVING RANGER

You must go below the surface to truly understand an emergency's hazards so that you can control your focus. If you do this properly, then you won't have to rely on others to make the scene safe for you. You and you alone are responsible for your safety, and it is critical that you make decisions that protect yourself. This is an investment well worth making because without it, you risk getting injured or killed and therefore unable to design your disaster.

Thankfully, the responders in the Yosemite resort drill didn't experience any of the negative repercussions I've outlined in this chapter, but they did learn a big lesson that day. Having a pile of five able-bodied responders laying in front of some wires because they weren't paying attention to their surroundings was a significant handicap as the drill progressed. At the end of the exercise, I ran upstairs to check on the group—we hadn't heard from them in a while, and since they clearly hadn't been evacuated out of the building, someone had to account for them. When I arrived at the second floor, the drill monitor there was standing next to the pile of "killed" responders with a sheepish look on her face. Next to her? The dog, who had fallen asleep.

Part Three

RESPOND

Conquer the "Lights and Sirens" Phase Using the C3 Method

Chapter Seven

EVACUATING, SHELTERING IN PLACE, AND LOCKING DOWN

On December 26, 2004, residents of Khao Lak, Thailand, realized that something very strange was going on. They heard very unusual shrieking coming from the elephants, normally calm and quiet, in a nearby wildlife area. This went on for hours, waking many of the residents, until suddenly the animals turned away from shoreland and began a massive stampede. People on the main street of Khao Lak darted out of the way as the elephants ran at nearly full speed. A group of villagers followed them to see where they were going. The elephants had managed to find the highest point on the island and were congregating there.

Knowing that something was obviously amiss, villagers and others later ran to the beach and looked down at the tide line, which was much lower than it would normally have been at that time. It was then that they suddenly realized something that the elephants had known for hours: a massive tsunami was coming.[41]

The 2004 Sumatra earthquake and subsequent tsunami that occurred in the South Pacific is considered one of the worst disasters in human history, claiming hundreds of thousands of lives and destroying billions of dollars of property.[42] The stories from that tsunami, however, have taught emergency managers important lessons in evacuations, saving many lives in disasters since. One of the most powerful of these lessons is that conducting an evacuation, shelter-in-place, or lockdown (ESIPL) quickly and efficiently is one of the best ways to save lives and protect property. However, in many disasters, the inability to conduct an ESIPL effectively (or to do one at all) has led to unnecessary risk. To design any disaster, you must learn exactly how to perform each of these in responding to disasters that you face.

In part one, I discussed how the C3 Method could be applied as you prepare yourself for a disaster event. Then I outlined for you how to translate that preparedness from panic to focus during the Gasp, the moment you recognize a disaster is occurring, by redirecting your energy. Now we move on to the part of the disaster cycle that is certainly the most visible: Respond. The response phase focuses almost exclusively on three things: life safety, incident stabilization, and property protection, in that order. While this is the stage where most disaster preparation is focused, it is the one that few truly understand how to conduct correctly.

Before I get into the problems typically associated with ESIPL, it is important to define each one completely, as there are many times when these terms are used incorrectly in the media and by various organizations.

- **Evacuation:** This is an ordered movement of people from one place to another to avoid the impacts of a threat. There are three types of evacuations: A *spontaneous* evacuation is one where people decide to evacuate without instruction from public officials during a sudden life-threatening event. A *voluntary* evacuation is when officials inform the public that it would be in their best interest to evacuate but make it optional to do so. Finally, there is *mandatory* evacuation, where an immediate threat to life and property exists, and public officials order people to evacuate an area to avoid the threat. Tsunamis, major hurricanes, and other regional incidents routinely result in mandatory evacuations.
- **Shelter-in-Place:** This is where conditions are such that people should seek protection inside a building or home, where they will be safer, when there is a threat outside. Severe storms and weak hurricanes typically result in a shelter-in-place. Even minor storms

can prompt a shelter-in-place. When I traveled throughout Florida as a young consultant, I can think of a dozen times when I sheltered in place with other grocery-store patrons when there would be a short, temporary downpour of rain so heavy that we would have to congregate near the doors. But as they say in Florida, "If you don't like the weather, wait five minutes." After the rain stopped, we would break our shelter-in-place and continue to our cars.

- **Lockdown:** The best way I can explain a lockdown is like this: no one in; no one out. A lockdown can be thought of as a hard shelter-in-place, where severe injury or death could occur by going outside; therefore, securing yourself inside becomes the best avenue. But this is not the same as a shelter-in-place. In lockdowns, doors and windows are secured and locked, and no one can go outside. It is not just safer to be inside; it is dangerous to allow movement in and out of the area under lockdown. Chemical spills, active shooters, and similar types of incidents are common lockdown scenarios. The start of the COVID-19 pandemic, when human-to-human contact was considered extremely dangerous, was essentially the largest lockdown in human history because quarantines are also a type of lockdown.

Many times, I'll get asked about a certain disaster and which ESIPL is appropriate for it. Of course, the answer can vary, but ultimately, in every disaster, no matter what form it takes, there are three possible responses. I don't care if it's an earthquake, a tsunami, a volcano, an IT disaster, a cyberattack, a terrorist attack, an active shooter, an insect swarm, an alien invasion, a public-relations crisis, or whatever else. It will boil down to an evacuation, shelter-in-place, or lockdown.

YOU HAVEN'T WORKED OUT THE DETAILS OF THE ESIPL

The first problem when it comes to ESIPL is that most people don't know the appropriate procedures to conduct an ESIPL in a way that maintains their control. Most of the time, people assume that the government will instruct them on when to leave and where. Or they just go off their "gut instinct." Both approaches can actually put you on weaker footing because, as stated in previous chapters, no two disasters are the same.

Even in professions where practiced evacuations are common, there can be very unexpected disasters. In 1980, Lake Peigneur in Louisiana experienced a very unusual disaster: an oil company was doing exploratory drilling for oil when it accidentally bored its fourteen-inch-wide drill bit into an active salt mine. Once the miners realized what was going on, they were immediately able to evacuate everyone out of the mine before they were all killed. However, when they evacuated (initially onto Jefferson Island), figuring they were safe, a massive whirlpool formed in the lake and began to suck the entire island itself down the hole—prompting a second evacuation.

We have all seen the videos and photos of freeways entirely blocked by evacuating traffic during an approaching hurricane. Details like alternate evacuation areas must be ironed out in advance—such as transportation, sheltering, and personal logistics—or the consequences can be severe.

For example, in February of 2022, Russia crossed the border into Ukraine, sparking a major regional conflict. One of the things that was interesting was that in the days prior to the invasion, the US State Department advised Americans to leave Ukraine immediately. The alert was very forthright, informing people that they needed to have their own contingency plan and that the US government would not be able to rescue them in the case that Ukraine was invaded.[43]

This kind of planning is also important in sheltering. Evacuees routinely show up at American Red Cross shelter sites carrying weapons, large animals, and other prohibited items and demand entrance. I have a hotel client in Northern California who, during a wildfire, took in evacuees who later refused to leave after bringing their dogs into their rooms. And hospitals, which can act as 24/7 shelters for employees during disasters, sometimes have to manage people who leave their pets in their cars. In multiple occasions, these animals have been left in the back of flatbed trucks and have bitten those who happen to pass by and startle the animals out of their sleep. More common are animals housed in the cabs of trucks with all the windows rolled down.

In all the above situations, you are not able to prioritize your actions properly. The result here is the same as with the previous disaster pitfalls: you tie your ESIPL success to someone else and leave control of your evacuation to various sheltering agencies—an unwise decision.

Leaving ESIPL solely to emergency management is a serious problem because when it makes a decision for you and you decide that it's *not* what you want to do, the resulting conflict can cause confusion that unnecessarily risks lives. This will limit your options, raise your dependence, and create risks to your family.

C3 METHOD SOLUTIONS

Famed martial-arts expert Bruce Lee had the perfect approach to this. When I was a brand-new black belt in Shaolin Kempo, I read Lee's book *Tao of Jeet Kune Do*. In it, he lays out his approach to dealing with complex and difficult situations. The book, which is written in a narrative style with a series of philosophical truisms, advises readers to "Be like water."[44] Lee explains that water adapts to every situation: When it's too cold, it freezes. When it's too hot, it turns to steam. When water is going over a brook, down a waterfall, or through a raging river, it perfectly contours to its environment. If you become like water, therefore, you'll be able to adapt your mind and body to any situation. I want you to be just like that in a disaster. Be like water. I want you to be able to instantly adapt to any situation, as ESIPL will require you to do. That mindset will put you in a position of maximum independence because then you won't need others to do everything for you. Adaptation requires that you give yourself maximum flexibility with maximum options, which decreases your dependency on one organization, government, or person.

COMMAND – "I CAN EMPOWER MYSELF"

As we've seen, if you don't take responsibility for your own ESIPL, you are carelessly risking your life and those of your family and first responders. Such a reliance on others takes you from an active to a passive state when designing your disaster. By inverting this pattern, taking Command, and placing yourself in charge, you can assert your own control over your own disaster ESIPL because no other agency will be in charge of it for you—not the sheltering location, the government, or your workplace.

This is the "Responder 1-2-3" rule I designed for my clients:

- If it's a category or level, add one (+1)
- If it's distance, double it (x2)
- If it's time, triple it (x3)

For instance, if you're facing a Category 3 hurricane, assume it's a Category 4. If authorities say a tornado is an EF3, assume it's an EF4. Why would you leave the safety of your family to fate or the unpredictability of nature? This doesn't mean you have to go overboard—if it's a blizzard, you don't need to assume the next Ice Age is starting. But you do want to slightly overestimate because that'll maximize your options.

As for distance, it's important that you give yourself a wide berth from the hazard. This is not only to avoid the imminent danger but also to prevent you from getting into crowds of evacuees. On the water, mariners estimate the potential movement of a hurricane in all directions. For any known path of the storm, they use a map to draw potential alternate paths of the storm 100, 200, and 300 miles in multiple geographic directions. By avoiding not just the storm's anticipated route but also the possible *un*anticipated paths, they never get into a position where they cannot escape from danger.[45]

For time, if officials say a hazard will be removed in twenty minutes, you can basically assume it's going to be an hour. That doesn't mean it will actually take an hour; it means that you should assume it will so that you'll have maximum options to get away from the hazard and the large crowds around you. These rules of thumb allow you to "be like water" and contour yourself to any situation.

Determine for yourself if you must evacuate, shelter in place, or initiate lockdown in the event of an emergency. Don't wait for anyone else to tell you. Your quick, self-initiated decision-making could potentially save your life. For instance, on 9/11, there were people who decided to self-evacuate even though over the intercom they were told to stay put.[46] They were the only ones who survived. Make your decision and then do it. Don't be ambiguous about it. Don't debate. You have to just get it done. Especially if you are a caregiver, have small children, or care for large numbers of pets, you need to begin planning how to evacuate them today.

A frequent question I get asked is whether people should evacuate, shelter in place, or go on lockdown for a particular disaster where they live. My standard answer is that I have no idea; it depends on the inflection point. But I can teach you how to determine that. There are many factors to consider (I could write a book just on this subject alone), which include but are not limited to the:

- Type of disaster
- Geography and demographics where you live
- Sophistication of the local emergency management agency
- Quality of local roads

Not only that, but you must consider elements specific to you, including any that would slow down a particular ESIPL procedure. But once you've assessed the above criteria and understand your three options, the choice will become easier. Regardless of whether you have planned or not, once you have decided what to do, complete this three-step process for your ESIPL:

- Decide *when* you will do it
- Decide *where* you will do it
- Decide *how* you will do it

In each of these steps, be sure to act in a way that ensures a rational decision-making process for yourself and your family.

COMMUNICATE - "I CAN EMPOWER OTHERS"

Communication is key during an ESIPL. In fact, it could be argued that Communication is the critical element that will make or break it because both where you'll go and how you'll get there are dependent on your surrounding conditions and the relevant agencies' responses. Don't try to do things blindly. You will be severely disappointed.

I was working for a large homeowner's association in an upscale neighborhood in northern Los Angeles. It had hired me to help clarify its evacuation policies. The people there had been victims of a large fire on the mountain behind their park just the year before. They had trouble with their cell phones because the bandwidth had significantly lessened. However, one thing that always seemed to work was text messaging. So I wrote that text messaging would be their primary communication method. The next time they had a wildfire, the group sent out hundreds of messages to residents throughout the area, and the evacuation went very smoothly. That is clear Communication.

Telling yourself that the government will handle Communication decisions for you turns yourself into a bystander. The government can act as an important adviser, but it can't and shouldn't make those decisions for you.

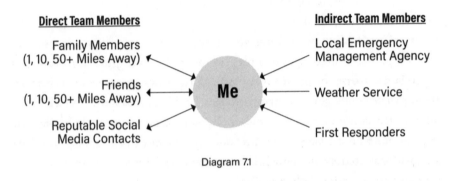

Direct Team Members

Family Members
(1, 10, 50+ Miles Away)

Friends
(1, 10, 50+ Miles Away)

Reputable Social
Media Contacts

Me

Indirect Team Members

Local Emergency
Management Agency

Weather Service

First Responders

Diagram 7.1

The direct team members you want to assemble are going to consist of people from your family, your friend group, and outside agencies. Assemble team members you can trust to help you, including those who can provide you with information necessary to guide rational, wise decisions. That way, you can make your own decisions and ensure that your ESIPL runs the way you want it to. For indirect team members, there is no question that government sources, first responders, and the news media, as well as online traffic apps (for evacuation), are going to shape what you do. For instance, in a tornado situation, you would rely on the local weather service and emergency-management agency to provide you with critical and immediate status reports on both the storm and current government and first-responder operations.

Once a decision has been made on how to act (evacuation, shelter-in-place, or lockdown), you must make sure to Communicate that decision to everyone who needs to know. Sometimes this is not an easy proposition. Cell phones might not be working, and other traditional means of calling through apps might not be feasible, either.

The reality is that if you don't pick who's on your team, the disasters will pick for you. You want people who know and understand your concerns.

CARRY OUT – "WE CAN EMPOWER EACH OTHER"

Now you must execute your ESIPL. You must plan your ESIPL out in advance to effectively carry it out when a disaster strikes. Contrary to popular belief, first responders can't always rescue you in a disaster when you need help. They aren't superheroes. They can't come down from the sky and help you in every possible circumstance. This is why you have to predetermine your plans in advance.

Evacuation

As mentioned above, evacuations are simply trying to get from one place to another, getting from danger to a place of safety. It's an organized, phased, and supervised dispersal of people away from dangerous or potentially dangerous areas. Evacuation is going to have two considerations: transportation and sheltering. Transportation is a major issue. In many disasters, those in vulnerable populations who can't travel on their own and haven't made arrangements for an ESIPL have to rely on home health companies, relatives, or others to secure a form of transportation. When available modes of transportation aren't equipped to deal with these kinds of people, evacuations can suffer major delays.

When are you going to evacuate?

This is not something you should try to determine by pure "gut instinct." I once was hired by a construction company to complete disaster plans for its various job sites. I'll never forget the plan I made for one such site in Bay County, Florida. I arrived to speak to the foreman and the contractor to write the disaster plan. They stared blankly at me as I talked about the company policies on evacuating for a hurricane. I informed them that, in the case of a hurricane, regardless of category number, the company required the job site to be completely evacuated. The two men then laughed. I started outlining this policy in more detail when one of them suddenly put up his hand dismissively. He refused to follow the policy and said that workers would be required to come in to work at his discretion *only*. When I tried to explain that this was a legal requirement and not my personal prerogative, he told me something I'll never forget: "Son, I don't even stop mowing my lawn unless it's a Category 3 hurricane or higher."

While I can appreciate his humor derived from experience, there is an ironic twist to the story. In 2018, Hurricane Michael went from Category 2 to Category 5 in just forty-eight hours, and I discovered later that that very same site we'd spoken at was completely demolished by the 160-miles-per-hour winds and that the hurricane completely flooded Bay County as well as the surrounding area.[47] Had that man called people into work shortly before the storm hit, there is no doubt there would have been significant injuries. In essence, he surrendered his own control of the situation to his past experiences. He let the past design his disaster. You can't do that. You must take each disaster individually and consider its danger on its own.

Where will you go?

To take Command, you must first figure out where are you going. There are three distances I want you to keep in mind: ten miles, fifty miles, and one hundred miles. In an evacuation, I want you to see your evacuation locations as being within concentric circles of ten, fifty, and one hundred miles from where you are. Try to think of an evacuation location for yourself, your family, or your business in each circle. *But no matter what, always have a primary and alternate location for your evacuation.*

From your house, you should arrange a place to go within the following mile markers: one mile or less, ten miles, fifty miles, and one hundred miles. That means that, in the vast majority of evacuation situations, you will always have a place to go. When I was growing up in California, where I experienced a number of major earthquakes, I lived next to a junior high school. My family established that if we ever had to evacuate, we would meet at the school's baseball field. Even in disasters like tornadoes, where there is very little warning, it is important to have an alternate location established for your family if your home is destroyed.

In 2012, when I was selected to be the US National Private Sector Representative to FEMA, one Friday evening there was a massive windstorm called a derecho that suddenly hit the DC area.[48] I had been in storms before, but this one came on with absolutely no warning, catching me off guard. It took out the power and caused significant disruption to the area. In fact, there was so much devastation where I was living that I ended up sleeping multiple nights in FEMA's headquarters, where there was power and a place to sleep (a couch near the office where I worked).

It's important to have an evacuation point fifty to one hundred miles away for major regional emergencies like hurricanes or large wildfires. In fact,

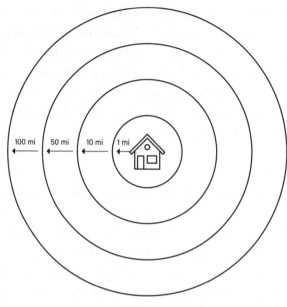

Diagram 7.2

during the 2012 wildland fires in Colorado, there were cases of residents having to evacuate more than 80 miles away. Wherever you plan to go, it should be at an appropriate distance for the kind of disasters you are likely to face. But identifying a location is only half of the equation. Getting there is the other half. When I lived in a small town near London, England, I used to ride my bike to the university. However, if we had a major disaster in the area, there was no way that a bike was going to be able to evacuate me and all the things I would plan to bring. So I made alternate plans with a local car company that would take me out of town if the buses and trains ever stopped working in an emergency.

How will you do it?

Transportation is an important consideration for your ESIPL. Transporting an animal or a dependent person, both of which may have unique transportation and sheltering needs, requires much prior preparation. If you work at a hospital or another emergency-response agency, you will have to coordinate with your employer. Don't assume everything will just "work out." Part of your responsibility as a caregiver, parent, or pet owner is to make sure you are working with appropriate organizations to safely evacuate *everyone* in your care. You don't want to leave this entirely to organizations or the government. You won't like how it will turn out.

Next, I want you to figure out how you are going to cover those distances. Are you going to take a car? Can you take a train? Is an airplane or helicopter an option? If you have a car, that's great. To make that work, however, you'll need enough gas, and you'll need to plan what to do if the car stops working or faces terrible traffic. During the 2018 Camp Fire, for example, there was a huge line of burned-out cars that ran for miles and miles outside of Paradise, California. People had simply abandoned them when they realized they couldn't get out fast enough.

I have also worked with families who own exotic animals; these animals can be very dangerous and require specialized handling. I once did some disaster work for an apiary (bee yard) in northern Oklahoma, and we had to determine how to evacuate literally thousands of bees. Arranging for trucks and determining exactly how to evacuate these bees safely was a large consideration. It took work and time, but we were eventually able to do it.

Shelter-In-Place

The second possible response, after evacuation, is what's called a shelter-in-place. A shelter-in-place is when you remain inside a protected area away from the hazard. Sometimes this is called a "reverse evacuation."

When are you going to SIP?

One day, when I was a brand-new emergency manager in Louisiana, I decided to go down to New Orleans to have a look around. As I was walked down one of the streets in the French Quarter, I was looking down at my phone while listening to a song. Suddenly, I felt a hand grab me by the shoulder and pull me away from the sidewalk.

Thinking I was about to be robbed, I yanked out my earbuds and prepared to fight back—only to be met by a friendly face who told me to get inside immediately. We were standing just outside a café, so I followed him inside. Fifty people stared at me as we entered. Before I could say anything, I saw a flash of lightning and heard a massive thunderclap like a cannon exploding. I almost jumped out of my skin. After getting my bearings, I proceeded to get a lecture from the café patrons about thunderstorm safety as the rain poured down. What I experienced that day was a very basic shelter-in-place. And I am very thankful to those people. I lived in Louisiana for a long time afterward, and the lesson they taught me served me very well.

You need to be able to determine when it is safer to be indoors than outdoors. That is the only rule. As soon as this is the case, it is time to SIP.

Where are you going?

You should always establish a primary and an alternate location within your home, business, school, classroom, or office where you can shelter in place. Doing so ensures that if a primary location isn't available, you'll have an alternate that you can go to. A primary location can be as simple as staying inside your home with the windows and doors fully closed and locked. But if a situation is more dangerous, you should have an alternate. Good areas in which to shelter in place are those without windows, without chemicals of any kind, and with easy access to exits and food.

When someone asks me to give a generalization of a good place in their home, I quote Associate Supreme Court Justice Potter Stewart in the 1964 *Jacobellis v. Ohio* case when discussing how to differentiate pornography from mainstream erotic art: "[I don't know, but] I know it when I see it."[49]

How will you do it?

You will go to that area and wait for the hazard to pass. It's really that simple. Once the hazard has passed, you either go back to normal, evacuate, or move into something more restrictive called a lockdown.

Lockdown

Lockdowns are very simple: no one in, no one out. They are essentially a preventative measure when a hazard outside a particular location is so dangerous that it could potentially kill or seriously injure you. Many times in the media I hear the terms "shelter-in-place" and "lockdown" used synonymously, but they are not the same at all. Shelter-in-place is when you are in a protected area to avoid a hazard. There is some freedom of movement, and there is no reason to believe the hazard outside is going to enter the building. Lockdowns, by contrast, secure you inside an area because a hazard might enter the building. There is a simple phrase I like to use when I am training people on lockdowns: "Nobody in, nobody out."

When are you going to go into lockdown?

The instant that it becomes dangerous to those inside and outside to allow anyone to leave. This could be because there is something you don't want to come inside, and for anyone to even try to leave would be dangerous for others involved.

Where are you going?

This depends on the kind of lockdown. If it's a security lockdown, go into a room that is lockable, throw everything in front of the door that you can, and call 911. If it's a contamination lockdown, pick an area—which could be your entire home—and then lock it up. If we are talking about airborne contaminants, this could be as severe as sealing windows with duct tape and putting down wet towels under doors.

How will you do it?

The most well-known type of lockdown is the one prompted by an active shooter, where we protect ourselves by locking doors, turning off lights, closing the blinds, and barricading ourselves inside. Then we wait for law enforcement to come get us. However, there are many other situations where a lockdown can occur, and lockdowns in these cases will look very different from those protecting against a mass shooter.

For instance, when there is a hazardous materials spill outside, you must lock the doors, close the windows, put towels at the bottom of the doors, and not let anyone come inside. The reason for this is because those who are outside may have already become contaminated and could bring that inside if let in. Another kind of lockdown is one the world is all too familiar with: quarantine. The COVID-19 pandemic highlighted the difference between an SIP and a lockdown. In a quarantine, you segregate yourself away from everyone to minimize the spread of pathogens from one person to the next.

I work with many outdoor resorts, and one lockdown that comes up from time to time is that for a wild animal attack. These can be serious lockdowns because sometimes they involve aggressive bears or mountain lions that have the physical ability to overpower any person and can forcibly enter a building.

In addition to these considerations, you'll need to decide who will be in lockdown with you. This may include:

- Caregivers
- Vulnerable members of your community
- Friends
- Employees
- Colleagues

If you're going to be in a lockdown or in a shelter-in-place, you must work with caregivers to ensure that anyone you are taking care of is protected. This is especially important if you're with people who are immobile, immunocompromised, or otherwise limited in their ability to travel far. Presumably, you will also want to ensure protection for your pets, since you won't want to leave them behind anywhere. However, do not at this stage concern yourself with objects, papers, and other material goods. Not yet.

Now that we have considered how you are going to ESIPL, it is time to consider the next two elements of the Respond phase of disasters: how to stabilize things and how to protect your property. Each of these is a critical part of modern living, and the steps you take to consider them will make a big difference in your disaster response.

WRAPPING UP: THE DAY THE ELEPHANTS RETURNED

In the weeks after the tsunami, the residents of Khao Lak came back to discover massive devastation of their homes and possessions. Many who had not heeded early warnings were lost; some were lost to the sea and would never be accounted for. However, those that took active steps after receiving the elephants' warning were able to maintain control of their own ESIPL and were able to design their disaster. In fact, many of the residents remained unsure upon their arrival as to whether the tsunami was truly gone. They had not received any information from the central government, and roads were still virtually impassable. So a few of them began to look for clear signs that the tsunami had passed and eventually noticed something: the elephants had returned.

Chapter Eight

STABILIZE THE DISASTER

W hen Viswanathan Anand, one of the best chess players in the world, left his home to attend the World Chess Championship in Sofia, Bulgaria, in April 2010, he was prepared for a short journey. However, on April 14, 2010, when the Icelandic volcano Eyjafjallajökull erupted, Anand found himself stranded in a foreign airport. Postponing the World Chess Championship was not going to be an easy proposition, but it was going to have to be done. Stuck in Germany, Anand went to a hotel, sheltered in place, and waited for nature to make its next move. After a couple of days of discussion, however, the International Chess Federation sent Anand a message explaining that even though the eruption was making travel difficult, it would not postpone the world-championship match.

Anand's team went into overdrive to get him to the tournament. The CEO of the company that sponsored the team offered his private jet. But because of the volcano, German airspace refused to let it off the ground. Next, they tried rental vans to drive them to Sofia. However, all of the rental car companies were out of stock due to the cancelled flights. They made call after call and determined that not a single car was available as thousands of other passengers vied for the handful of stock. Then the team looked into taxi services around Germany. However, all refused to drive the over-one-thousand-mile route from Frankfurt to Sofia. Finally, after some hours of scrambling, Anand and his team

were able to find two vans from a VIP taxi service to get to Bulgaria. The team
members, relieved to finally be on their way, celebrated, confident that Anand
would get to his match on time without any further hitches—until they realized: they didn't have Anand's luggage.[50]

Now that you have made the decision to ESIPL, you must stabilize the disaster.
Stabilizing disasters is something I don't hear enough talk about. You may have
determined where you are going to go, where you are going to shelter, how
you will get there, and even when you plan to return, but if you don't stabilize
the disaster, you will remain incredibly weak and ill prepared. Stabilization is
therefore a critical element in your disaster response because it helps to decrease
dependency on an organization to stabilize things for you, which will turn you
into a bystander who needs that organization as the hinge of their successful
disaster response.

   Stabilizing a disaster involves equipping yourself with all the physical and
digital items and resources you will need to sustain yourself throughout the
incident. These items fall under six categories of items, or what I call "the 6Ps."
Five of these were originally developed by FEMA, but I have added a sixth
category (and some detail to a few of the others). Each of these categories represents a set of items that are critical to have during an incident of any kind.
The categories are:

- Pharmacy
- Papers
- Personal Needs
- Professional Needs
- Priceless Items
- Pets

   I will go into each of these in more detail in the "Carry Out" section of this
chapter, but in essence, these are the critical items (and furry family members)
that you will need to maintain your physical, mental, social, financial, and professional health during an emergency.

NOT COMPLETELY STABILIZING YOUR LIFE DURING THE DISASTER

Disasters are going to create a measure of instability in your life. There's no doubt about that. The time duration of that instability remains up to you, however. Far too often, I see people who are seemingly prepared for disasters do so little to stabilize their response. Scrambling at the last minute for medications, a beloved pet, or a priceless item makes it so that you lose complete control of your disaster response. But the fact remains that since these items are critical to our lives, we must account for them when we conduct our emergency responses.

Failing to stabilize your life will lead to a compounding disaster. This is especially true if you get hit with a secondary incident. For example, the 2005 Atlantic hurricane season was the most active in US history, with more than twenty-seven named storms. The residents of New Orleans not only had Hurricane Katrina but also Hurricane Rita, as well as a series of other, smaller tropical storms.

In fact, that year they had so many storms, they ran out of names for them and used Greek letters—reaching all the way to "Z." Individuals who lost their identification or medication had to wait for months before they could access government services requiring ID. Those requiring basic social services also found themselves out to sea for an extended period of time and were under the complete mercy of government institutions to provide them. This exacerbated existing socioeconomic struggles, and many were simply unable to recover afterward.

What these people did not realize is that when you don't plan, you completely surrender control over to the government and other organizations. They made the mistake of not designing their own disaster. Many times, people are under a mistaken impression that a disaster will work out on its own. Hurricane Maria in 2017 was one example of this: people figured that the power would simply return back on when the government promised it would.[51] When it didn't, private corporations tried to step in, but when further storms rolled in, this proved to be destabilizing and made the problems of evacuees even worse. These kinds of compounding disasters create a magnified negative effect not only during extended incidents but also as people try to recover and build resilience afterward.

C3 METHOD SOLUTIONS

The 6Ps are the baseline of your disaster response, much like the six categories of chess pieces: the king, the queen, rooks, bishops, knights, and pawns. So, in a way, you can call them your "6 (P)ieces." Each piece is critical to your success in the disaster. Like chess pieces, each one has its own unique attribute that contributes to your overall success strategy. When you lose one, you become dangerously dependent on everything else to make up the difference. Losing a piece decreases the available strategies and advantages each one affords you and increases your dangerous dependency on someone else to provide them for you.

COMMAND - "I CAN EMPOWER MYSELF"

To take Command of a disaster stabilization, you must shift your mindset to a place where you are taking sole responsibility for it, much like a chess player does during a match. During a chess tournament, there is no texting, no life-lines, no help from the audience or coaches. It's just you and the sixty-four squares on the chessboard. In a disaster, people tend to want to surrender every-thing to the hands of fate or of government agencies, but it may very well be that you are totally on your own. I want you to make a single assumption when you are trying to stabilize a disaster: *that not a single person, organization, or government agency is going to help you.*

Yes, I want you to assume that you are all alone. That doesn't mean you will be. But this will require you to accept that if you do not stabilize the disaster on your own, no one else will do it for you. Pretend that you are on a desert island, and a big storm just passed over you. I want to force you to maintain a proactive mindset: *your 6Ps, your disaster.* You must maximize your options.

COMMUNICATE - "I CAN EMPOWER OTHERS"

The team you assemble must assist you; get as many people involved as possible to support you as you determine which items must be taken with you, which will help you plan your actions. While I will cover who some of those individ-uals might be for each of the six categories, it's important for you to consider what information sources are most relevant to you.

For instance, if you take a regular prescription and are going to be evac-uating more than one hundred miles, you must make sure that you have enough medication to take with you or that your pharmacy will be available near where you are headed. If you have a pet with specific needs, you'll need to call ahead to make sure wherever you are sheltering will allow you to have your animal with you. If you are bringing your laptop with you and doing sensitive work, it will be important to verify that the internet you will be using has a secure line and doesn't run the risk of having data stolen or making you vulnerable to cybercriminals. When you do this type of advanced stabilization preparation properly, you'll no longer be relying on others to meet your needs. I use an example here of what your team might look like if you have to evacuate your pets:

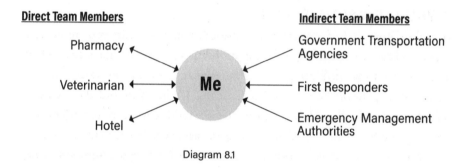

Diagram 8.1

Sometimes people ask me about whether my philosophy is still true for those considered vulnerable. My answer: this is *especially true* if you are vulnerable. For example, during Hurricane Irma in 2017, Manatee County Emergency Management held a televised news conference with an American Sign Language (ASL) interpreter who was supposed to help relay critical emergency information to deaf viewers. However, it was discovered almost right away that the interpreter was unqualified. Some sentences were gibberish or totally nonsensical. While emergency-management officials went over important evacuation-guideline information, the interpreter signed, "Pizza want you are need be bear monster" and "Toys for who Mexican."[52]

To counteract these kinds of issues, it's important to develop backup ways of receiving information. While it is the expectation that the government will provide you with perfect information every time, you must remember that dependency on a single line of information decreases your resilience—because if that one source fails, the rest of your response will be in jeopardy. The way to be truly prepared for a disaster is to avoid a single line of dependency and to increase your own self-sufficiency.

CARRY OUT – "WE CAN EMPOWER EACH OTHER"

We now must gather our 6Ps and put ourselves in a place where we are prepared for what we are dealing with now—and for the potentially extended incident that might come. A shelter-in-place or lockdown situation can easily turn into an evacuation, so you should prepare yourself to gather items in each category even if you are only sheltering in place at the moment. Here are those categories again, for your reference:

- Pharmacy
- Papers
- Personal Needs
- Professional Needs
- Priceless Items
- Pets

Now let's talk about each one in depth. At this point, you should decide what can be taken from each of the categories, but don't start gathering them yet!

Pharmacy

A pharmacy is incredibly important because of its obvious potential impacts on your physical health. This category not only includes prescription drugs but also any over-the-counter medication you may need, eyeglasses, oxygen tanks, or medical supplies that you need at all times. When you are evacuating or dealing with a long-term lockdown, you need to make sure that you have access to your pharmacy or someplace else where you can get additional supplies. One of the big problems that sometimes occurs in large-scale disasters is that diabetics can't get access to appropriate amounts of insulin. During floods or sudden earthquakes, large quantities of supplies can be easily destroyed. Since this is a critical medication for them, many times this is an issue of life or death. When proper planning isn't done, they are basically relying on the government or the local hospital to provide them with what they need.

Papers

Without a doubt, one of the single largest issues after a disaster is the procurement of personal papers. Government agencies after major disasters like tornadoes and floods are inundated with requests for replacement driver's licenses, Social Security cards, and even passports. This has become such a problem worldwide that the World Technology Forum in 2018 specifically discussed biometric identification in its challenges for the next twenty years.[53] For instance, in the days after Hurricane Harvey, identification (papers) became a major problem, as many residents had left them in their homes, which were destroyed.[54] This left them unable to access other financial resources or to replace credit cards or ATM cards that might have gone missing. Therefore, ensuring that you can access the 6Ps is essential to putting yourself on track to designing the disaster.

In addition, private companies are often asked to help replace critical loan documents and other legal documents that many times are lost in a disaster. This leads to yet another problem—after major disasters, the IRS routinely audits people in disaster areas because of the prevalence of fraud in claiming repair deductions.[55]

The way to handle this is to put an expired driver's license in your emergency backpack. Remember how I mentioned in chapter three to have an empty pocket in your disaster backpack? Your papers are what I want you to put in there. These are critical documents that can make or break your disaster response and can be the difference between stabilizing the disaster and not. Personally, while I do have an expired license in my disaster backpack, I also always have my passport in the pocket of my emergency clothes that I would be wearing if I ever had to evacuate my home. It is zipped up and very well protected. When I travel, I always keep my passport on me. A passport is an internationally recognized document and can easily get you any other identification that has been destroyed in a disaster.

You don't have to lug around all your other papers, but for any that you truly care about, you should have a digital and hard copy. These might include deeds to homes, loan documents, and even medical records.

Priceless Items

What I am referring to here is anything you think is so critical, you can't leave without it. These include photo albums that haven't been digitized, keepsakes, and anything else that would be irreplaceable and have a dramatic psychological effect on you if lost. However, this does *not* include large valuable items like furniture, large paintings, or your massive collection of *National Geographics*. I address these in chapter nine, as they must be considered separately from the items that you can take yourself. I don't think a further definition is necessary. The only person who can define these items is you. What I will say is that you must make sure they fit and are not prohibited by wherever you are planning to shelter.

Personal Needs

I could probably spend a dozen pages writing out every personal item you might need in a disaster. There are some obvious things to start with: keys, a wallet, a purse, a cell phone. However, instead of simply just giving you a list, I want to give you a new way to think about this category. I want you to get items that are important for your physical, mental, and spiritual well-being. These don't have to be religious items; they're anything that make you . . . *you.*

No matter what, grab your emergency backpack (customized for you, I hope) and include toiletries, clothes, and any other items that you'll need in a separate bag. Don't forget basic items that will help you with the logistics of a disaster, including your cell-phone charger.

Professional Needs

Consider what you might need to contact your workplace—or actually do your work—during a disaster. This might include a laptop or tablet, phones, or other technological equipment. To make this sync up, though, you are going to have to Communicate with your workplace to ensure that what you have is sufficient for remote work. There have been instances where firewalls have blocked cloud access from employees when they are trying to access via a virtual VPN while at home. This is a common anti-hacking technology. If you are working as a teacher or in a capacity where you must interact with people on a daily basis, you might need to secure things like high-speed internet or hard copies of important documents.

Pets

For us pet parents, our pets are our family. I have lived with many cats in my life, and every single one I considered an important (although sometimes taciturn and moody) family member. I may have your pets last on the list, but it's only because I want you to consider something important: if you are going to design a disaster for your pet family, just go through these 6Ps with them in mind as you would with any other family member.

For instance, in the first weeks of World War II, 400,000 animals were euthanized in Great Britain alone in preparation for a potential invasion from Nazi Germany. Given the short notice provided, the Home Office's National Air Raid Precautions Animals Committee met on August 23, 1939, and created a pamphlet for people to read about how to take care of their animals. They advised people that if animals could not be transported, they should be euthanized humanely before being killed by invading troops or bombs from above.[56] While this advice would be considered abhorrent and largely unnecessary today, there have still been situations when animals have been neglected or left behind during a disaster because organizations simply couldn't handle the volume of animals coming through their door. There is a simple solution: plan ahead.

Pharmacy: Start with your pharmacy and ensure that any medications your animals need are considered. When one of my cats got an eye infection, we had to refrigerate her eye drops. If I had needed to evacuate my home, I would have had to make sure she had her drops in a cooler.

Papers: Make sure you have any appropriate ownership paperwork. One item that is always important is identification. If you become separated from your pet and it is rescued by an emergency animal-rescue service, there may not be an easy way to identify you as the owner. Take a photo with your animal in your home. Make sure the photo clearly shows that it was taken where you live.

Priceless Items: I would include that one toy or bed your animal can't go without. These items are important to them and would have a negative impact if missing.

Personal Needs: These include everything you can think of for day-to-day care, like food and water, toys, leashes, and harnesses. But also take some treats. It is important to keep up their spirits as much as anyone's.

Professional Needs: For your service animals, take their vests and paperwork, as they will be "on the job" during a disaster. If you are one of those rare people whose animal has a job in public (like if they are a YouTube or social-media star), or if your animal is a professional show animal, be sure to take anything they will need, like specialized combs or collars. Then, post about it online to encourage others to do the same. Demonstrating your animal's disaster preparedness is something to share!

If you have a dangerous exotic animal, like a Komodo dragon or something, then the job is going to be complex. You will have to consider where you will take the animal and whether its required supplies are ones you can take with you. For instance, if you have a fish tank, it is unlikely that you will be able to take your fish with you. That means you should prepare a shelter-in-place for them by getting EST that allow them to stay where they are.

In an ideal condition, you should determine what your 6Ps are in advance and put them in writing within a disaster plan. Your plan should include a simple set of instructions and priorities that will strongly aid you as you gather the needed items into a single unit. If you haven't done this yet, it's perfectly fine! So long as you're not currently in a panicked mode (and are in a focused minset instead), you can do this very easily within a few minutes.

In the case of an evacuation, you have to consider exactly how you will transport your items. Remember, you can't bring your Komodo dragon on an airplane, and you can't fit your grandfather clock in your car. You'll have to make decisions, much like a chess champion does during a match, since there is a finite amount of space on the board for your pieces: eight pawns, two rooks, two knights, two bishops, one queen, and one king. You might wish you had ten queens and only a few pawns, but that's not how the game works. Disaster responses are just like this. You have to make sure that what you are selecting fits onto your "board."

When you maximize your pieces and think through your limited space ahead of time, you can do what you want. By coupling your ESIPL decision with a prioritized set of personal items, you can stabilize any disaster for yourself.

WRAPPING UP: CHESS CHAMP IN LIMBO

As you have read, stabilizing a disaster means more than simply evacuating out of an area or finding shelter in your home. It involves a comprehensive examination of the 6Ps in your life to ensure that you are able to regain control of the incident and not turn it into a disaster. When you do this, you will be in a position to focus yourself and minimize the disruption that will characterize the experience of others. In fact, if done right, you will set yourself up for the ability to make yourself even stronger after the incident is over.

Team Anand understood this as it sought to take the World Chess Champion to his tournament in Sofia, Bulgaria, in 2010. They were able to finally get a car, make all the visa arrangements, get the drivers in place, gather Anand's luggage, and even find entertainment for the trip (the *Lord of the Rings* film trilogy). But as they were entering the Bulgarian capital, they were caught driving over the speed limit and were pulled over by a Bulgarian police officer. They figured that this would be another major problem and that it might lead to additional complications with Anand's visa, perhaps preventing him from getting to the match on time. However, the friendly police officer, after learning who the famous passenger was, just smiled and said, "Okay, take him to Sofia." Then he paused. "But not too fast, okay?"

Just a few days later, on May 13, 2010, Anand beat home-favorite Bulgarian Veselin Topalov and successfully defended his world-championship title. When Anand and his team got back into the van after the tournament, preparing for their long journey back, they turned on the third *Lord of the Rings* movie, *The Return of the King*. It seemed fitting, watching the two young hobbits successfully escape Mount Doom—an exploding volcano.

Chapter Nine

PROPERTY PROTECTION: YOUR LAST PRIORITY

I was once hired by a large conglomerate to write a disaster plan for a mobile-home community in Arizona, and the community manager told me a story about the maintenance coordinator, who'd had to evacuate with his family when a wildfire threatened the park. As they were packing up the car, he began watering his roof to protect it from the embers that were being showered on it. One of his neighbors, in his own car trying to evacuate, asked him if he would water his roof as well. He agreed and hosed down the neighbor's roof. Then a third resident in the neighborhood who was about to leave asked him to hose down his roof, too.

This continued until the maintenance coordinator had watered about a dozen roofs in the neighborhood while his family waited patiently in the car. All the while, ash and embers were floating around them. Finally, a deputy sheriff who had been blaring an evacuation order on his loudspeaker saw what was going on and asked him why he was still in the park. The maintenance coordinator explained to the sheriff that he was watering the roofs of people's homes. The deputy, concerned with his safety and that of his family, threatened him with arrest if he did not evacuate the park with his wife and children.

During a disaster, it's only natural that we would worry about our property. A raging wildfire or a dangerous tornado will lead us to the inescapable prospect that we could lose items that matter the most to us, from our home itself to a priceless old photo album or even our laptop. There is nothing wrong with this concern, except that many times this results in our taking unnecessary chances with our lives to protect these things. When we don't create a categorized prioritization of our property, we basically surrender it to forces outside of our control. Therefore, it is critical that we develop a clear mechanism for protecting these objects while at the same time ensuring that we are not overly prioritizing them. Otherwise, we are letting objects dictate when and how we leave.

NOT PRIORITIZING CORRECTLY

Far too often, people risk their lives for property. On some level, I can understand this. Our homes are important to us, and we accumulate objects, mementos, and tools of modern living so that we can live comfortably. The problem becomes when we do this in a way that risks our lives and those of our families and friends. Protecting what seems like an invaluable material possession can sometimes needlessly risk your life.

When you don't properly prioritize these things, your possessions will control your disaster response. Because these things matter to you, they quickly turn into a dependency and lower your capacity for resilience because they limit your options. If you won't leave your house, now you can't evacuate. If you are worried about an antique bench your grandfather built, then you're going to be racked with indecision. If you have weapons you want to carry with you, you can't go to a public shelter. If you have a lot of technology that you know isn't backed up or that you are unwilling to leave behind, you will have to spend precious time deciding what to do with them. This is costly in moments when minutes and hours may make all the difference.

The first thing to know is that *nothing is worth your life*. If you have gathered the 6Ps from the previous chapter, then the vast majority of what you will need has been accounted for. At the same time, however, it is naïve for anyone to just tell you to drop everything you have without a care in the world.

I am going to show you how prioritize correctly with the C3 Method. By completing this process, I will give you a simple, fast set of questions to ask for each piece of property in your home or business. These questions, when completed through the C3 Method, provide a powerful methodology so you can sort through each object quickly and with confidence.

C3 METHOD SOLUTIONS

I wrote the chapters for the Advanced EMT textbook on disaster response, and there is a section where I cover responding to mass-casualty incidents. These are instances where there are large numbers of victims and very few EMS professionals on hand to help them, such as a train derailment or a large car-accident scene. In these instances, EMTs have to use a system to make snap decisions on who to treat first and who needs the highest medical attention. This best allows the EMTs to focus on who needs them the most. It also allows them to Communicate this information to responders who will arrive later. We call this process of prioritization "triage," which comes from the French word meaning "to sort."[57] This is a rapid process where the EMT should spend no more than thirty to sixty seconds on each patient. Essentially, there is a set of four questions each EMT must answer as they evaluate each patient.[58]

When I train EMTs on triage, I take them out of the classroom and then fill the room with teddy bears. Each teddy bear has a note card around its neck that provides the EMT with the four critical pieces of information that tells them how each "patient" is to be prioritized. I also put up a timer and make sure that there is barely enough time to finish. If the EMTs don't complete the prioritization process within the allotted time frame, I ring a loud buzzer, take them out of the classroom, rearrange the bears, and have them start again until they have it down cold.

I want you to adapt a similar process for your property when you are in a disaster situation. I want you to triage every item you have. *Your possessions are the teddy bears of the disaster response.* I am going to give you a triage tool that will allow you to spend no more than thirty to sixty seconds on each item. This is a powerful methodology that will help you sort through each object quickly and with confidence. I call it the "Property Triage System" and have used this effectively with businesses and families for a long time. It is a simple tool that fits perfectly into the C3 Method and makes it easier to prioritize all the property in your home during an evacuation.

COMMAND - "I CAN EMPOWER MYSELF"

Before I get into the method, we must have our mindset in a proactive, ready state. When it comes to your property, there is a simple way to take Command over it. Shift your mindset so you assume that *if you don't triage them, you will either lose your most valued possessions or risk your life for useless junk . . . or both.* Protect your property on the basis of this assumption alone.

Psychologically, this gives you an edge because it puts you in a place where you've done what you can for every item—and then that's it. You now assert your own control over your own disaster prioritization. What it also does is give you power so that you aren't overwhelmed by the task, since there are so few people but many possessions. Much like with the teddy bears, you will have to make quick, critical decisions about your property, but you first must realize that the only way to determine what priority needs to be taken toward each item is by applying a consistent methodology from start to finish.

Too often, I see people trying to save every little item or throwing objects into their cars to save them from a raging wildfire or incoming hurricane. This is a mistake because not only are you likely to miss something important, but you may also find that you wasted valuable time and space on objects that could have been easily replaced or protected. Focus and apply a methodological process to your possessions.

COMMUNICATE - "I CAN EMPOWER OTHERS"

When I train the EMTs on triage, they don't work alone. I pair them up so they work in teams of two. One person does the triage; the other puts a tag on the "victim" to signal to other responders what the priority is for that patient (the tags are green, yellow, red, and black). That second person also keeps an eye out on all the patients, cues responders as new ones arrive, and helps the EMT with the triage if they get stuck. The pairs do this for a dozen or two bears, and then they switch roles so that each responder gets the chance to triage and to assist. Your triage will be exactly like that—you will need other people to help you correctly sort your property. However, that doesn't mean you won't have any indirect team members. If you have something insured, you should look at your insurance policies to make sure that they are still covered. This will help in the decision-making process.

CARRY OUT – "WE CAN EMPOWER EACH OTHER"

First, do *not* risk your life for *any* object. *Ever.* There is nothing that is worth your life. We love our photo albums that haven't been digitized, our prized collections, our treasured written journals, our laptops and tablets—but in no instance is it worth it to put yourself in harm's way to retrieve these things.

There is a way to protect your property: make someone responsible for it. For every item, select a person to be responsible for it in a disaster. If you categorize your items in this way, in an emergency, you won't have to worry about any of the items that you assigned to others. Someone else will have *Command* over those items. Ideally, prepare for this in advance by including these assignments in your disaster plan. But if you can't do that, follow the Property Triage System when you face a disaster. It's pretty easy, and you should be able to finish the entire thing in about ten to fifteen minutes.

The system is going to give you a tremendous advantage because what it will do is assign Command over each item to someone. It will diffuse the responsibility so that every object that matters to you will be accounted for. As mentioned above, in the EMS triage system, we have four categories for patients: green, yellow, red, and black. However, for your Property Triage System, I am going to give you just three categories:

- Replace it
- Secure it
- Transport it

Each of these categories will provide you with a clear mental framework for your items. As you go through the questions in the Property Triage System, it will become very apparent how you should take care of each set of objects in your home. This system will decrease your dependency on anyone else because it gives *you* the power to prioritize your possessions and determine what will happen to each one of them.

The Property Triage System

Now it is time to prioritize our property. Whatever you end up doing, do not overreact and try to grab everything you consider priceless. Instead, for every item, I want you to go through this three-question questionnaire. These questions will help you assign people to take Command over each object in your home.

You can mark your items with anything you want, but I recommend using green, yellow, and red. Just use tape.

1. Can it be replaced? (Green)

- If *yes*, then stop here. Give Command of it over to the insurance company.
- If *no*, go to the next question.

If it can be replaced, then move on. These items are not worth wasting your time over because, while you might be sad to lose them, you can still replace them and therefore shouldn't worry about them. Examples in this case are:

- Cookware (I love my cookware, too, but it can be replaced)
- Furniture
- Clothing
- Appliances
- Food
- Large exercise equipment

For these kinds of items, you are handing responsibility to the insurance company or to fate if they are destroyed. This doesn't mean that you have to forget about them; try to catalogue them quickly, since you'll want to replace them eventually. You should do what you can to catalogue all of them via video. This type of evidence will help when you are doing insurance claims after the emergency. If you can, shoot a video on your phone of everything to prove what you have. For lots of items at once, I use a GoPro helmet to capture a full accounting. It's not going to be perfect—you're not going to be able to include and capture everything—but this avoids risking people's lives and maximizes your limited time.

Look—I love my Xbox, but I'm not risking my physical health so I can play an *Assassin's Creed* game. That'll only add to the physical, emotional, and mental challenges to recovery post-disaster.

2. Can it be protected or secured in place? (Yellow)

- If yes, then stop here. Secure it in place.
- If no, go to the next question.

If it can't be replaced, then we must see if we can protect it or secure it in place. In this case, we don't want to leave it to fate or to the insurance company. So we'll have to check if we can protect it either by securing it where it is now or by relocating it somewhere else. Examples include:

- Antiques
- Trophies and awards
- Technology (large)
- Weapons
- Books and artwork

Depending on the size of the item and the disaster you're facing, this may be as simple as putting a blanket over it or moving it to an area of your home that is more protected from the hazards. Interestingly, a bathtub is a pretty good place to put objects because of the strength of the tub and the tiling around it. Of course, you will want to put plastic over the object, as well as a blanket, if possible. Other good places are on beds or in closets.

3. Can it be transported? (Red)

- If yes, then stop here. Find a way to have it transported.
- If no, then specialized handling may need to be arranged.

The last question is whether the item can be transported. In other words, can be it evacuated? If the item is small enough, you might be able to place it in your emergency backpack. However, in most instances, you will need to have some other way of moving it.

But what if it can't be transported? What if you have something that isn't replaceable, can't be sheltered in place, and can't be transported? This comes up a lot with families who have collections of valuable objects that can't be transported normally, like wine bottles that must be in a temperature-controlled environment, or require specialized handling, such as valuable artwork, or are particularly delicate, like musical instruments.

The point is that this evaluation must be done *quickly*. You won't have hours and hours to spend on this. Do what I train the EMTs to do: ask the questions, then move on. Thirty to sixty seconds. That's it. Next, next, next. The tempo is going to be extremely important because it's easy to get bogged down in details or specific items. Fortunately, most items can be replaced, leaving you more time to focus on those items that are important to protect or transport.

For these items, identify a specific place to move them. Examples of such items include:

- Jewelry
- Valuable Books
- Technology (small)
- Money
- Exercise equipment (small)

I've seen people who own large amounts of antique items, firearms, or coin collections really struggle with this part of the prioritization process. They want to take those things with them, but they can't be transported easily or quickly for one reason or another. Don't let difficult-to-transport items hinder your evacuation! Plan ahead and make arrangements so that if you can't transport them yourself, and you can't shelter them, and they aren't replaceable, you aren't put in the position of having to decide between your life and a valuable collection.

I once had a client who had a large collection of music paraphernalia. He adamantly told me that he would not evacuate his home without it, no matter what. I told him this was fine as long as it didn't put rescuers or his own life in danger. So what we did was create a detailed plan for each item in this collection, including where it would go and how we could retrieve it after a disaster.

Remember, there is a difference between *wanting* something protected and *needing* something protected. I'm a known book lover with a rather large book collection. I own thousands and thousands of books. But I know I can't take every book with me in an evacuation, sadly. So I need to have a prioritization plan in place. I'll take the few books I know I won't be able to replace, and I'll leave the rest.

Before you evacuate, you should also do some basic protection for your home, whether that's unplugging appliances or making sure to board windows and sandbag doors, depending on the disaster at hand.

If you are evacuating at the last minute, don't try to save everything. It's tempting, but don't do it. You don't have the time. Set a time limit of seven minutes per room, maximum. You can even send children and other family members to their own rooms to begin their own assessment and help speed up the process.

By applying the Property Triage System, you won't assume that someone else will handle the appropriate prioritization of your property, and you'll ensure that you won't be risking your life over material things.

WRAPPING UP: WET SHINGLES BURN, TOO

The items that adorn our homes and give us pleasure in our lives are an important consideration in any disaster. Whether a valued photo collection, an old trophy, or a dried-up rose from a long-remembered first date with a significant other, it is important that we catalogue and determine which items can come with us, which must be secured where they are, and which will be left to the hands of fate. If you apply the Property Triage System to everything you own, it will provide you with the peace of mind to rationally decide what you will do with each of your items. This three-step method can be applied quickly and easily, allowing you to design any disaster.

After the wildfire in that Arizona mobile-home community, the maintenance director came back to the park with a corporate and insurance representative to conduct a Preliminary Damage Assessment. He had taken substantial risk to himself and his family when they were evacuating to try to save the homes of the people in the community with his simple garden hose, and he was looking forward to seeing the results. As they entered the park, they went to the street where the houses had been. Home after home on that block had been burned to the ground. Despite all his efforts, not even one remained standing.

Part Four

RECOVER

**Restore Your Life in Five Sentences
Using the C3 Method**

Chapter Ten

PART ONE OF THE SENTENCE: WHAT NEEDS TO BE RECOVERED?

D uring a massive volcanic eruption, the curator of Iceland's Skogar Folk Museum had a decision to make: which items to take with him. It was a difficult decision, as there were more than fifteen thousand objects spread throughout the building. However, after an hour of consideration, he grabbed just one object. It was a book from 1584 that had been purchased by a local parish—a Bible that had been beautifully inscribed. In Iceland, a country of nearly 400,000 with near-universal literacy, it was considered one of the most prized possessions of the museum. After grabbing the book, the curator ran out of the building.

Now that I have defined for you how to prepare yourself for a disaster (Ready), how to deal with the first moments after a disaster strikes (React), and how to get through the "lights and sirens" phase of disasters (Respond), it is time to focus on Recovery.

The first thing to remember is that a disaster *always* passes. The question is . . . how quickly can we get it to pass for you? Let's start by defining disaster recovery. Disaster recovery is the ability to restore your basic life functions so that you can continue to live your life after a major incident like a blizzard, cyberattack, or building collapse. That's it. It identifies what you need to live. As you will read below, this is more than simply food, water, air, and shelter.

Disaster recovery focuses on you as a complete, functioning person in a modern society: psychologically, financially, professionally (or educationally, if you are still in school), and socially. Up until now, disaster recoveries have not focused on these areas as a collective whole.

What's important is not the disaster itself but how we decide to design our own recovery. You can design your recovery so that you are in charge and in control. That is going to be very different from what you may have read in any other disaster book. I've used my revolutionary technique with clients around the world with tremendous success, and I think it will work for you as well. What I am going to propose to you in this chapter is a brand-new way to think about your recovery. I want you to know that you can recover from anything in your life, and you can do it quickly—even in the face of a massive disaster.

RECOVERY VERSUS "RETURNING TO NORMAL"

For too long, I have seen disaster recoveries that have been started improperly. Too many people try to get their lives back to normal before they have fully recovered from a disaster. While this statement may seem nonsensical to you, it's a serious mistake that is made all the time.

Before I go any further, I think it is important to differentiate between "recovery" and "returning to normal." These are *not* synonymous. Recovery is about getting life back to a place where you can function day to day. The focus is on you and your physical, mental, and financial health, as well as the basic functions needed in a modern society. There is a narrowly defined set of baseline personal functions that sustain you each day.

However, "going back to normal" is a comprehensive set of activities that will get your life back to the way it was—like trying to get your home fixed to its pre-disaster state, buying a new TV to replace the old one, getting your carpet cleaned. These are all important, but it won't prevent you from living your life to not do these things, unlike if you are ill and unable to get critical medication for yourself. For right now, I don't want you to focus on going back to normal. I want to focus on getting you in a place to function at all.

There is a significant temptation to immediately start jumping into "getting back to normal." But this is a dangerous for several reasons. There is an old adage that says, "If you chase two rabbits, you will lose them both." If you haven't yet recovered your basic life functions, what's the point of trying to call the insurance company to get money for your possessions? No amount of insurance money is going to help if your health is in jeopardy.

Some will try to rush you quickly into getting back to normal when you aren't yet recovered. The biggest offenders are generally insurance companies. Like the government, the insurance industry has a big part to play in getting you back to normal, but it will play little to no part in helping you recover. Most insurance policies do not cover temporary housing stays or temporary living expenses, regardless of what you may see in commercials. Their *only* job is to help finance your loss for replaceable items; they can't get you back to physical or mental health and can't put you back into a place where you can operate day to day.

Beyond that, "getting back to normal" before you recover from a disaster will wear you out, and you won't end up doing either. Plain and simple. "Getting back to normal" can take months or even years to complete. In fact, depending on a variety of factors, it may very well be that you will never get back to normal. I argue in chapter thirteen that this can actually be a tremendous advantage to your life, but if you don't recover first, you will lose this golden opportunity. The tempo of recovery is fast; the "getting back to normal" pace will be much slower.

By trying to define what "normal" is before completing your recovery, you miss a tremendous chance to change your life for the better. Hurrying to get everything back into place essentially admits that there was nothing to learn from the disaster and that no other opportunities have presented themselves as a result when, in fact, you may need to make some massive changes to your life to make yourself more resilient for the next one! I'll discuss this in more detail later, but what I want to emphasize now is that we must first get you into a place where you can recover the basic functions of your life so that we move you back to "normal" later.

I believe the reason for these false starts at recovery is mostly innocuous and unintentional: most people simply don't know what they need to recover.

But if you don't know what you must recover, how will you be able to recover anything? Recovery is more than just finding a roof over your head. It is a systematic examination of your life to determine what you need in every area of your life.

Often, we think getting our house back into pristine condition is recovery. It's not. You want it back, yes. But do you *need* it back right away? Let's say your house is back in pristine condition, but you've neglected your mental health or now suffer from chronic financial or professional problems that could have been headed off with a few practical steps. Does having your house back in perfect order really make any difference then? Are you ever going to be able to get past the disaster this way? The difference between disaster recovery and "getting back to normal" can be distilled in the example of your home. If your house is destroyed, do you have a place to shelter? That's disaster recovery. Do you have all your furniture back exactly where it used to be? That's "going back to normal."

Modern living is now sophisticated, but basic life functions for humankind have remained remarkably steady. It is only now, though, that we have more sophisticated tools and strategies to address them. During most disaster recoveries, however, you can quickly complicate your life by trying to address every detail of your existence.

When you prioritize "getting back to normal," you make the same fundamental mistake I see in all kinds of disaster situations: you assume that someone else will handle your disaster recovery for you. Either you think that it will happen naturally (it won't) or you rely on another organization, another person, or another government agency to handle it on your behalf. This happens constantly, particularly in large disaster responses when there is a lot of media attention.

Sometimes people will leave their recovery up to aid organizations like the American Red Cross and other nonprofits. When I was on a Disaster Action Team in Louisiana, I went to house or apartment fires where large numbers of people were displaced. While we were often able to get them into temporary housing, this was not a long-term solution. Many were shocked to have hotel vouchers for only a short time. They thought we would rehouse them for a long time when this was simply not realistic.

Don't hand off your recovery to the government or another organization— because if you rely on them for sheltering, food, water, equipment, supplies, money, or other resources that fit your unique needs, you are going to be disappointed. They can't customize a recovery for everyone. The greatest analogy I can come up for this situation comes from the hit '90s TV sitcom, *Seinfeld*. In the episode "The Nap," George is put in charge of "Fitted Hat Day" at Yankee Stadium by his boss, New York Yankees owner George Steinbrenner. He laments at his bad luck and yells at Jerry, "Now I gotta figure out the hat sizes of 59,000 different people! What if a pinhead shows up? I gotta be on top of that!"[59] This is exactly what the government has to do when it provides services to a population affected by a disaster. The chances that it will run out of metaphorical hats in your size are extremely likely. The government does some things very well—and other things not so well. One thing it has not proven to be very adept at is recovery.

The other organization people often leave their recovery to is their workplace. Your workplace may have many great things about it, but it may not be able to recover you. For instance, if the company you work for is not able to recover itself within thirty days, and you need a paycheck within fourteen days, you'll have an asymmetry of sixteen days' worth of money that you must account for in a disaster. You will have to ask hard questions. This is something that really should be addressed pre-disaster—after disaster strikes, it might be too late.

When you leave it to someone else or another organization to recover you, what you are doing is significantly increasing your dependency on them. This will make your disaster recovery significantly more difficult because you will have tied your resiliency to that organization and instantly transformed yourself into a bystander. If they don't have a fitted hat in your size, then you're totally out of luck. They are now designing your disaster.

C3 METHOD SOLUTIONS

Over the next three chapters, I am going to outline for you an immediately implementable framework for recovery that you can use in literally any disaster, whether it's a tornado, massive fire, or cyberattack. And I am going to do it with just one sentence that we'll break down together. This is something I have done for thousands of people. I call it the "One-Sentence Recovery," and it's a simple and easy tool to help you recover.

The One-Sentence Recovery is very powerful because it will help you define exactly what you need without any frills or unnecessary extras. I developed this sentence years ago when I started working with families and small businesses, and now I am going to share it with you. You won't find this sentence in any other disaster book anywhere in the world. *This is the most powerful disaster-recovery tool ever developed* for people like you because it allows you to develop your own "fitted hat."

COMMAND – "I CAN EMPOWER MYSELF"

Do not let any other agency try to recover you. As you proceed below and identify the areas of your recovery, assume that *if you don't identify a recovery area yourself, you will never recover it.* By choosing that mindset, you become empowered to design your own disaster recovery. Recovering yourself will define everything else you do throughout the rest of the disaster. That is why it is essential that you take charge of it and Command every element of it.

COMMUNICATE – "I CAN EMPOWER OTHERS"

As I have noted in prior chapters, the only purpose of Communication is to organize a team. There is no question that you will need to leverage various people and organizations during a disaster recovery. They will help you identify not only your areas of recovery but also what you will likely need to make those recovery areas successful.

There will be a lot of Communication necessary here. We're not just talking about family. Be ready to speak to a wide range people in your life who can advise you. Communicate as necessary with each of these people and determine whether you have enough support to access the necessary resources for your recovery. However, don't expect your team to be perfect. Remember, we are only laying out the groundwork for your recovery.

One issue that sometimes comes up in recovery is when you are so overwhelmed, you can't think straight. Here's an easy solution to that: implement the buddy system as you recover. Have someone you trust and who you know will support you and be honest with you act as your recovery buddy. In hazardous-materials management (hazmat), we do this all the time. When I would put on the big alien suit (called the "Level A"), I always had a partner who would keep an eye on me during the shift, and vice versa. If I started to look unwell or began to experience unusual symptoms, I had someone who could react and ensure my safety. You should do the same. Have a buddy (a friend or family member) keep an eye on you so that someone can monitor your personal welfare and safety while you are recovering post-disaster.

CARRY OUT – "WE CAN EMPOWER EACH OTHER"

You must lead your own recovery. Every step you take, and every element of the recovery that you perform, must be 100 percent led by you. No other government agency or nonprofit can get you the "fitted hat" that you need to complete your disaster recovery. That responsibility lies with you. This doesn't mean these kinds of organizations don't play a part in your disaster recovery. However, in the end, you are the one who must take charge.

You are now on your path to defining your disaster recovery. Let's define your "fitted hat."

DEFINING YOUR RECOVERY SENTENCE

When you complete the One-Sentence Recovery, you will be in a position to recover yourself in any area of your life. We are going to break down this sentence into three parts. In this first part, you will learn what you must recover. In chapter eleven, you will learn how fast you must recover, and in chapter twelve, you will discover the strategies necessary to complete the sentence.

Let's begin. For any element of your life, if you want to recover it post-disaster, you want to complete this sentence:

"To recover my _____ health, _____ must provide access to _____ in _____ days and cost _____."

This sentence is so powerful because it defines what you want to recover, what elements we need to recover it, what strategy we're going to employ, how much it will cost, and how quickly we must do it. Each part of this sentence represents a critical part of your recovery. We're going to take it piece by piece. By the end of it, you will have a recovery strategy you can use every time. In some disasters, you will use this sentence for one or two of the recovery areas. In others, you will use it for all five. You can use this sentence over and over.

Furthermore, you can use this sentence for yourself, for your children, for a vulnerable person you are assisting, and even for your pets. I have also used derivatives of this sentence with small businesses around the world. We don't have room in this particular book to discuss how you could apply it to every possible situation, but I will say that this sentence can easily apply to a wide variety of organizations and people.

The reason why recoveries most often fail is because those affected by a disaster don't take one of the aspects of the Recovery Sentence into consideration. So let's go step by step, identify each element of your recovery, and unlock your potential to recover quickly and easily through a possible real-life scenario.

SCENARIO INTRODUCTION

It has been a dry September, and the city where you live has experienced a major wildfire. You work in an office that is under threat, so you and your colleagues leave early. The smoke and danger of fire has forced you to evacuate from your home, as that is under threat as well. You are not alone; you are also evacuating your school-aged child. You have successfully packed up the car with everything from the 6Ps and have driven to your Aunt Cheryl's house, who lives about one hundred miles away and is out of range of the fire. As you unpack the car, you begin to construct your One-Sentence Recovery.

PART 1 - "TO RECOVER MY _____ HEALTH"

The sentence starts like this: "To recover my _____ health." This isn't much of a sentence so far, but this is the easiest part because there are only five possible answers. Each one is important in ensuring that you have what you need to recover post-disaster. Here, we're simply designing what needs to be recovered. Each person is going to have their own recovery and their own needs, and I'm going to help you to define exactly what those needs are. They are:

- Physical Health
- Mental Health
- Social Health

- Financial Health
- Professional Health

These areas are critical to your recovery because they represent the simplest areas of your life. Let's start with physical health.

Physical Health

When I discuss your physical health, I mean food, water, shelter, clothing, and medication. This also includes any medical attention or rehabilitation that is necessary for your survival. Physical health encompasses all of your immediate and long-term medical and physical needs.

For example, if you are immunocompromised and go in for regular injections, or if you get dialysis or breathing treatments of some kind—these would all be considered part of your physical health. Also consider any emergency medicine you need on hand at any time. If you are prone to anaphylaxis, you may need to have access to an EpiPen. In a disaster, you may not have all of your protein powder, but you'll want to make sure to cover your immediate needs.

Mental Health

Mental health obviously involves the psychological aspect of your person. I am not simply talking about your immediate mental-health needs in a disaster but also your long-term psychological resilience. If you have a condition like an anxiety or panic disorder, you will have to consider it as you recover. Every person is going to be different in this regard, so the question I ask generally is: What do you need to cope?

Some of the coping mechanisms here could include therapy, medication, or inpatient treatment—whatever you need to help you during a triggering event like a disaster on top of any current treatment you are receiving. Ignoring this is a serious mistake. For instance, I once worked on a disaster plan for a drug and alcohol treatment center in Southern California. When I spoke to the director, she told me that if the residents ever had to evacuate, they would be back on the streets. She told me (as she was a recovering addict herself) that if the facility closed in a disaster, the first thing they would do is abuse drugs and alcohol again.

Mental-health trauma can appear in many forms. During the sarin-gas attacks in Tokyo subways in 1995, five thousand people presented themselves to hospitals, claiming to experience symptoms. While only a fraction had really been exposed, the rest were psychological casualties we call the "worried well" that overwhelmed hospitals and caused significant disruption to the health system.

Financial Health

Financial health in the modern age is obviously a critical recovery target. We must have access to credit and cash during a disaster. It's also an issue of ensuring that you can get credit extensions and emergency money when traditional financial institutions are not available. Like it or not, Madonna was right: we are living in a material world. So having uninterrupted access to financial instruments is critical to the fight—once again, not to get back to normal but to ensure that you have access to the financial resources you need during an incident. How much money are we talking about? We will address that in the next chapter.

Social Health

When I talk about social health, what I mean is everything that makes up who you are socially, like your circle of friends and family. Maintaining access to your social networks (and not just digital ones) can be a critical link between your physical and mental health. This might also include going to the gym or having access to a quiet place to meditate. If you are religious or spiritual, it could mean going to a house of worship. Whatever makes you feel centered, gives you a sense of purpose, and gives your life meaning falls under social health.

This can even include clubs like the Rotary and Kiwanis clubs or personal groups and hobbies. A close mentor of mine and her husband were members of a Corvette club that took recreational drives every weekend to a different destination. They would drive the few hours to the place, have lunch and socialize, and then drive home. For them, this was an integral part of their lives.

Professional Health

Your professional health (or educational health, if you go to school) involves anything you need to ensure that you can continue to work or go to school. Schools these days have developed more sophisticated mechanisms for ensuring the continuation of day-to-day education amid obstacles, particularly in the wake of the COVID-19 pandemic. Distance learning and e-learning are just two of these.

At your workplace, you want to make sure you are continuing to do what you must to get a paycheck and maintain the financial infrastructure you enjoy as a result of your job, such as health insurance and other benefits, particularly if you are an hourly or contract employee.

Each of these elements of your health should be given equal importance based upon what you know about yourself. Taking Command means taking responsibility for what your values are and what you will need in a recovery.

So let's return to our scenario. You've arrived in a safe location, so you're out of the Respond phase, and you are now developing your One-Sentence Recovery. You have food, water, air, and basic sheltering. You are fully functional; however, you have a chronic medical condition that requires you to take a certain medication every other day. Your doctors have warned you on multiple occasions that missing your medication even once could jeopardize your health.

Your mental health is average. As a result of some childhood and adult traumas, your mental health is strongly dependent on psychotherapy because you deal with acute panic attacks and depression. You're not on psychotropic medication, and you don't have an emotional support animal. For the moment, you have a few important photographs that are helping you cope because they are reminders of better days and help comfort you during times of great stress and panic. But you've been in regular therapy and have been meeting with your licensed therapist once a week.

You've lost some contact with your friends, but the internet is working where you are, and because you are staying with a relative, you have access to family. You're still not sure about work, but you have credit cards and cash to survive. Plus, Aunt Cheryl bakes one heck of an apple pie.

You work in a small business office as a supervisor and are responsible for five employees. Your boss is the owner of the company. From the start of the COVID-19 pandemic, you worked remotely, but you've recently returned to the office.

Based on this scenario, three areas of your life have been directly impacted (or interrupted) by the wildfire.

- Physical Health: Not recovered
- Mental Health: Not recovered
- Social Health: Recovered

- Financial Health: Recovered
- Professional Health: Not recovered

Already, you have recovered two of the five, so you're doing okay so far because you have access to critical social connections, as well as to the financial resources you need. So, right now, you only need to work on three sentences for your disaster recovery to be successful. Here they are:

- "To recover my physical health, _____ must provide access to _____ in ___ days and cost _____."
- "To recover my mental health, _____ must provide access to _____ in ___ days and cost _____."
- "To recover my professional health, _____ must provide access to _____ in ___ days and cost _____."

Now that we have established the health areas that have been affected, we're actually going to skip the next blank and come back to it later. So we move to this: "must provide access to ___." For each of the five areas of recovery, we must determine what we'll need to ensure full functioning in that area. Below, I have provided some suggestions for each area on what this might include, but you might have ones of your own. Again, we're not looking for what will make everything go back to normal—we just want to make sure you can function.

Physical Health
- Food
- Water
- Clean air
- Exercise
- Shelter
- Sleep
- Medicine
- Specific medical treatment(s)

Mental Health
- Medicine
- Therapy
- Animals
- Connection with others
- Books
- Coping skills

Financial Health
- Cash
- Access to credit
- Work
- Other financial income streams

Social Health
- Friends
- Hobbies
- Religious services
- Meditation

Professional/Educational Health
- School
- Corporate email
- Access to corporate cloud drives

Again, these lists are *not* comprehensive—but if there is something here that's applicable to you, add it to your own lists! If you do this comprehensively for every area of your life, you will be able to quickly recover each one.

In our example scenario, two of your five areas have been totally taken care of: you're fine financially and socially. Great. But you're working on recovering your physical, mental, and professional health.

Let's apply our lists to each of your areas. You need access to medicine (physical health), therapy (mental health), and high-speed internet (professional health), so now your sentences should read like this:

- "To recover my physical health, _____ must provide access to medicine in ___ days and cost _____."
- "To recover my mental health, _____ must provide access to therapy in ___ days and cost _____."
- "To recover my professional health, _____ must provide access to high-speed internet in ___ days and cost _____."

Perfect. In completing this exercise, you've made this problem so much easier. Instead of trying to blindly get back to normal, you know exactly what you need to recover each of your three impacted areas. Do you see how much simpler this is than worrying about your house or whether the insurance company is going to pick up the phone? Don't worry about those things currently. Right now, you need to focus on *you*.

I want you in control of your own recovery, and you have now taken that first step to creating your "fitted hat"—without a reliance on the government or an outside agency to do this all for you. The key, however, is to make sure that you are being comprehensive. If you have to speak to your doctor or to a work adviser for support in getting what you need, that is what they are there to do. Remember that the government and nonprofits will guide you as to what kind of recovery you will need to perform. But they won't do it for you.

WRAPPING UP: START SMALL

Determining what you will recover is the first critical step in your disaster recovery. It gets you back into a place of basic functioning so that you'll have what you need to keep yourself going. You can complete the Recovery Sentence multiple times for multiple people, and it will cover exactly what you need to design any disaster. Remember to take your time and determine which of the five health categories are going to be most relevant to you.

Now that we have determined *what* we need to recover, we must determine *how quickly* we must recover those things, and at *what cost*.

Back in Iceland, when the curator returned to the museum after the eruption, he was asked why he had selected the Bible to take with him. He answered: "You don't feel starving or in pain if you have a book."

Chapter Eleven

PART TWO OF THE SENTENCE: DETERMINING THE TIME AND COST OF YOUR RECOVERY

April 18, 1984

Dear Mr. President,

My name is Andy Smith. I am a seventh-grade student at Irmo Middle School, in Irmo, South Carolina.

Today my mother declared my bedroom a disaster area. I would like to request federal funds to hire a crew to clean up my room. I am prepared to provide the initial funds if you will provide matching funds for this project.

I know you will be fair when you consider my request. I will be awaiting your reply.

Sincerely yours,
Andy Smith

This letter was received by the White House just a few days after being sent by middle-schooler Andy Smith to then US president Ronald Reagan.

Considering the level of seriousness ascribed to this project, one can only imagine what his room must have looked like! While we look to this letter today as quaint, it has some tremendous implications because Mr. Smith (even though only a middle schooler at the time) seemed to have understood a critical disaster-recovery concept: recovery takes time and costs money. His request for federal matching funds was a recognition that money is a major consideration when we determine how to initially get ourselves functioning after a disaster.

In the previous chapter, we began the initial program of recovery, defining what needs to be recovered. But now that we have done so, we must think about Andy's letter: How much is this really going to cost? And how long is it going to take? I'm sure Andy's mother wasn't going to wait around for the Army Corps of Engineers while his room remained a "disaster area."

The first thing to know is that the longer recovery takes, the greater the cost will be. This is especially true if you have a special vulnerability. When you are designing your disaster, your time and cost elements are critical. They are so important that if they are not defined precisely, your chances of successfully recovering after a disaster will plummet significantly. What you will be left with are few, if any, options, which will force you to be at the mercy of another agency or organization to recover you. They don't know you. They don't have a "fitted hat" for you.

By this point, you have begun your recovery, you have established your Recovery Sentence, and you have begun filling it in. That's a good start.

You can now move on to completing the details of your recovery. In this chapter, you are going to determine how quickly you can recover and how much it will cost. This will help narrow the scope for what options are available to you. Remember, the Recovery Sentence in its entirety is: "To recover my ____ health, _____ must provide access to _____ in ___ days and cost _____."

YOU DON'T KNOW HOW LONG IT WILL TAKE TO RECOVER

Defining the time necessary for the recovery gives you a powerful filter to determine your options. It is critical to know what your deadlines are in a disaster. If you don't know how long your recovery will take, you can't make the right decisions. Therefore, your needs for how quickly your recovery *must* take need to be aligned with your actual options of how long it will take. For example, if you need to take a particular medication every two days to avoid serious repercussions and your supply is low, you'll have to make sure that your pharmacy will be open within your needed timeframe. That means, in practice, that your recovery time has to be aligned with the number of current doses you have and when the pharmacy might reopen after a disaster.

Another example is in the professional world, where your livelihood is completely tied to the survival of the organization you work for. You may need a paycheck every two weeks, but if your company does not reopen or has a policy tied to performance or attendance, you could be in real trouble during a disaster because your livelihood will be dependent on its decision to reopen.

This is not theoretical. Workers around the United States got a taste of this during the COVID-19 pandemic, when many companies had to tell employees they would not be returning to their brick-and-mortar workplaces for an indefinite period of time, which had a major effect on employee salaries and benefits. Therefore, appropriately aligning your timeframe for recovery is just as important as identifying what your recovery is. When your timeline for recovery doesn't match up with your realities and needs, you will become completely dependent on outside organizations, which will decrease your resilience when you may need it the most.

YOU DON'T KNOW HOW MUCH IT WILL COST TO RECOVER

Disasters cost money. That seems a basic truism these days, but it is a critical factor in determining your recovery options. Cost is probably the biggest problem in most recoveries. What you think may be available may not be because it may be financially out of reach. And in a disaster, if you don't have access to your traditional mechanisms of financial control (cash, cards, digital wallets, etc.), recovery can become slow. It's important to determine the cost of what you have available at the time of the disaster. This will help further refine your options.

No one is expecting you to do a major balance sheet for your disaster recovery. It's unnecessary unless your life is exceedingly complex. But you do have to at least determine the upper limit of what you will be able to afford and what finances you will have access to. If you don't, the first thing that will happen is that you are going to leave your disaster recovery to someone else—because you will either run out of money, run out of options, or both. This is not an unusual occurrence. During Hurricane Sandy in 2012, Ocean City, Maryland, was hit so badly that banks throughout the area were closed for weeks. Electricity and cell-phone towers were also unavailable for an extended period of time. Lack of access to money and other resources meant that many people could not purchase basic supplies, even though they could have afforded them in normal circumstances.

You have to define your budget, but you can make adjustments to it as you work on your Recovery Sentence. For instance, I once worked with a family who hired me to custom-design its disaster recovery. I went through each of the five recovery areas with them. When we began discussing professional health, the parents told me they both needed to be on call and available at all times. So we established their recovery time at 0:00 (as in, they had to be recovered instantly). After reviewing their options with them, I told them that while I could recover them that quickly, it would cost them $100,000 per year (for satellite phones, mobile uplinks, predetermined and set-up office locations, etc.) They were shocked—so they said, "Well, maybe not that fast." After going back with this new information, I determined that I could get them back professionally in about three days at a cost of $1,000 a year. To them, it was worth it. To you, maybe it isn't. That is going to be completely dependent on you and your lifestyle.

You must determine: Are the consequences of not recovering within your desired time period worth it? Or is meeting the recovery deadline worth paying the money for? Imagine, for example, you have to have physical therapy (PT) once a week for an injury from a debilitating car crash you experienced earlier in the year. If you miss your weekly appointment, you get increased pain and swelling that makes it difficult to sleep and conduct daily living tasks. Now imagine your city had a flood and the office where you normally did your PT was closed and would be for four weeks *at least*. Let's say you found another PT office, where an appointment would cost $200 more, but they would see you that very week. The question for you then becomes: Will you pay the extra $200 a week to meet your physical recovery goal, or will you keep the $200 a week and accept the pain and swelling that will inevitably accompany the missed appointments?

When your physical or mental health is in jeopardy, saving the money may not be worth it. But these considerations are highly personal. You decide what your physical and mental health are worth.

C3 METHOD SOLUTIONS

COMMAND - "I CAN EMPOWER MYSELF"

The first thing you must do is realize that time and cost are the two most import-ant elements in determining how your recovery can be conducted properly. You have to assert control over both by accepting that *if you don't identify the time and cost to recover yourself, you will never recover.* Don't try to simply do this off the top of your head. You have to perform a systematic examination of your life to determine exactly when you must have an area of your life recovered and how much you can spend to do it. When you leave this to guesswork, it's like you're a bystander in your own recovery because you are acting with only partial information (or none at all). You don't want to leave this to anyone else because they won't follow your timeline. They will follow their own.

COMMUNICATE - "I CAN EMPOWER OTHERS"

Communication is critical. Whether you are speaking with your doctor, your workplace, or your child's school, you have to ask questions to evaluate the con-sequences of certain actions so you can make the most reasoned judgment. This doesn't mean that you need to contact every person in every area of your life. Instead, you should first perform a self-examination of what the consequences would be if you didn't have access to something. Afterward, you can empower others to help you because they will be able to give you the information you need to make these critical decisions. Unfocused Communication, however, will not give you any advantage and will likely hinder your ability to determine the exact time and cost of your recovery—which will require much Communi-cation and a lot of information. We are going to rely on the same team we had before to help us decide what we need for cost and time determinations.

CARRY OUT - "WE CAN EMPOWER EACH OTHER"

In our example scenario, you fled your home as a result of a raging wildfire and decided to shelter safely at a relative's house one hundred miles away with your family. Your financial and social health are just fine. However, we have deter-mined that you must recover your physical, mental, and professional health.

Since we last worked on this sentence, let's pretend that you have heard from your workplace, a professional office. Your boss, the CEO, has informed you that the office has closed for the indefinite future and that everyone will need to be in an online meeting in two days to see where they are. Of course, the CEO wants you to have access to high-speed internet so that you can get into the appropriate corporate platforms with a clear connection. You told the CEO that you have your laptop with you and that you will be in attendance. With this information, we can now return to your Recovery Sentences:

- "To recover my physical health, _____ must provide access to pharmacy in ____ days and cost _____."
- "To recover my mental health, _____ must provide access to therapy in ____ days and cost _____."
- "To recover my professional health, _____ must provide access to high-speed internet in ____ days and cost _____."

At this point, you may notice that we haven't discussed anyone else's timeline. That's because we don't care. At all. We only care about *your* timeline.

Now we must work on the time and cost portions of your Recovery Sentences. Let's start first with how fast you need to recover.

DEFINE START AND END DATES

The first step of any disaster recovery is determining when it will start and when it will end. You'll want an exact date when the recovery will begin. The best rule of thumb I can give you is that the day you are no longer in *immediate physical danger* from the disaster itself is the date you should set to begin your recovery. The end dates also need to be well defined, to provide a clear goal for completing the recovery, and I will discuss how to do that, too.

The way to do this is to assume that if you *don't* set a start and end date for your recovery, your recovery will never start and never end. For instance, after the 2019 Notre-Dame fire, recovery authorities determined a precise date for the full restoration of the cathedral in 2024. This provided them with a clear goal and a definable deadline. By setting these dates, you begin to assert your own control over your disaster recovery. In business continuity, we call the end date the recovery-time objective, or RTO. Again, when you set an end date, it won't be the day when everything goes back to being the way it was. It's just when you'll get back to a baseline of functioning effectively post-disaster. Importantly, this date is not moveable. Set the date and stick to it. Then set goals for your recovery. These goals will be significantly more meaningful with a completion date in mind.

Determining the time you need to recover is critical. It not only influences our end recovery date but also modifies our options to be able to recover in the first place. So how quickly do we need to recover? We can find out by determining the amount of time you have left until serious repercussions occur. Repercussions include physical damage to yourself and any other adverse condition financially, socially, etc.

Let's take an easy example: everyone needs water. The longest a person can go without water is just three days.[60] For food, it's roughly thirty days for the average person (but a vulnerable person or one with dietary requirements won't last nearly as long). If we were to apply this to a Recovery Sentence, it might read like this:

- "To recover my physical health, _____ must provide access to water in three days and cost _____."

So, at a minimum, our recovery time would be three days for water. If we don't obtain water within that timeframe, we risk severe dehydration and other life-threatening complications.

If you work an hourly job and live on a precarious financial edge, let's say that you'll have to return to work within five days of a disaster. If you don't get in at least thirty hours within that first week, you're looking at financial ruin. So your recovery time would be five days to recover your professional health. Of course, each of these numbers can change for you depending on the disaster and its conditions.

Now let's return to our example scenario. We now know that to recover your physical health, you'll need access to a medicine for your chronic illness in two days. We also know that you need access to licensed therapy for your mental health. The question is: If you are in therapy, how long can you go without it before there are repercussions? I have some clients who tell me that they must have access to their therapist every day. Then I ask them if they do daily therapy, and they admit that in reality, they only meet once a week. That's a big difference. Then I ask them what the consequences would be if they didn't have access to their therapist for more than one week.

What about a month? I try to get them to stretch so that I can find the upper limit of how long they can go without their therapist. That is their RTO. You should do the same—ask yourself how long can you go without something before there are serious consequences. And by serious consequences, I mean anything that you feel would create unreasonable pain or irreparable damage to some part of your five areas of health.

In this scenario, let's assume you need to see your therapist every week; otherwise, you risk falling back into some unhealthy behaviors, which could have a negative effect on you outside of your mental health. The situation with your professional health is a lot simpler because your company gave you an exact timeline for recovery: in two days, you have to be in a meeting, so you'll need high-speed internet by that time.

So our example sentences become:

- "To recover my physical health, _____ must provide access to my medication (or a pharmacy) in two days and cost _____."
- "To recover my mental health, _____ must provide access to therapy in seven days and cost _____."
- "To recover my professional health, _____ must provide access to high-speed internet in two days and cost _____."

This is a good point at which to adjust your original end dates for recovery as needed, having now put together timeframes for each recovery area. In our example, we have determined that, based on the information we have, you need to be fully recovered in seven days. And now that we have determined the amount of time you have, we are in a better place to determine the cost of your recovery.

COST

Cost is a critical implication; therefore, we must now evaluate how much money you'll need for your recovery. Cost can be highly personal and sometimes completely subjective. How much are you able and willing to pay to meet your recovery deadline? Returning to our example scenario, what if I told you that I could give you access to a therapist in four days, but it would cost you $500? $1,000? $10,000? All of this will be contingent on your insurance copay and other personal factors that only you can know and would be impossible to list here.

You must assess how much you are willing to pay to avoid the negative consequences of not seeing a therapist in seven days. Let's say in our scenario that it normally costs you $30 per session to see your therapist because of your insurance coverage. However, if the therapist isn't available and you have to fig-ure out a way to get into therapy quickly, then that number is going to change.

Let's say the maximum you're willing to pay to see a therapist (yours or a different one) within seven days is $200. Furthermore, you're only willing to pay a total of $400 per month. After all, this is just a recovery therapist until your regular therapist returns (to normal rates) after recovering from the disaster.

So your new sentence becomes: "To recover my mental health, _____ must provide access to therapy in seven days and cost $400 a month."

For your physical health, the cost consideration is relatively simple; you need to get access to your medication as quickly as possible, and you're willing to pay $50 per bottle with a copay.

For your professional health, however, we might have a problem. Where Aunt Cheryl lives, there is no cell coverage and the internet is extremely slow. Her definition of a "social wall" are the photos of the family sitting on her man-tle, and the only streaming service she's ever heard of is one that sends fishing boats to the local river. This will all, of course, affect the cost of what it will take to get high-speed internet in just two days. Let's say you have a budget of $100 to find a place away from Aunt Cheryl's house with high-speed internet and cell coverage. Again, it doesn't mean you will actually spend $100; it just means that any option can't *exceed* that.

- "To recover my physical health, _____ must provide access to my medication (or a pharmacy) in two days and cost $200."
- "To recover my mental health, _____ must provide access to therapy in seven days and cost $400."
- "To recover my professional health, _____ must provide access to high-speed internet in two days and cost $100."

WRAPPING UP: BE EMPOWERED BY KNOWING YOUR PERSONAL NEEDS

Determining the cost and time of your recovery is going to be critical as you develop your recovery strategies, as this will provide you with a filter with which to evaluate each of the options you develop. President Reagan understood these limitations on strategies and was able to help young Andy Smith determine what federal resources would be available for his personal "disaster recovery" of his messy bedroom:

May 11, 1984

Dear Andy:

I'm sorry to be so late in answering your letter but, as you know, I've been in China and found your letter here upon my return.

Your application for disaster relief has been duly noted but I must point out one technical problem: the authority declaring the disaster is supposed to make the request. In this case, your mother.

However, setting that aside, I'll have to point out the larger problem of available funds. This has been a year of disasters: 539 hurricanes as of May 4th and several more since, numerous floods, forest fires, drought in Texas, and a number of earthquakes. What I'm getting at is that funds are dangerously low.

May I make a suggestion? This Administration, believing that government has done many things that could better be done by volunteers at the local level, has sponsored a Private Sector Initiative Program, calling upon people to practice voluntarism in the solving of a number of local problems.

Your situation appears to be a natural. I'm sure your mother was fully justified in proclaiming your room a disaster. Therefore, you are in an excellent position to launch another volunteer program to go along with the more than 3,000 already underway in our nation. Congratulations.

Give my best regards to your mother.

Sincerely,
Ronald Reagan[61]

Now that we have successfully determined what needs to be recovered, how quickly we must recover it, and how much we can spend on the recovery, we now must review our options to determine what strategies are available to us to recover the critical processes of our life—personally as well as professionally. What are our options for getting our mental and professional health back on track? Let's finish our sentence and design our disaster.

Chapter Twelve

PART THREE OF THE SENTENCE: STRATEGIZING YOUR RECOVERY

On January 17, 1994, at 4:30 AM, Southern California residents were rattled out of bed during a massive 6.7-magnitude earthquake. The epicenter was in Northridge, California, but the damage was spread over eighty-five miles. The twenty seconds of shaking, representing almost two g-forces, destroyed buildings, split freeways in half, and leveled entire city blocks of homes. One of the most affected institutions was California State University, Northridge (CSUN). Being immediately in the epicenter, the outside of many of its buildings were cracked, windows were broken, and power lines were laying on the ground.

Determined to reopen quickly before the semester began, CSUN began to strategize. But there was a problem: all of the buildings in the university were "red-tagged" by government authorities because they had to go through a structural-engineering evaluation prior to being entered again. So, for each of the critical processes of the university (student records, HR, classroom instruction, etc.), the school evaluated multiple strategies. Teams worked eighteen hours a day for more than a year and a half, working to recover every university process. Because CSUN did not have a disaster-recovery plan at that time, it was incredibly difficult to determine these strategies, which were limited by the circumstances.

Recoveries are disempowering states for most people because they have never taken the time beforehand to determine the strategies they must employ to complete a recovery. Not accurately and systematically determining your needed strategies leaves your recovery to someone else to handle.

While your life is not as complicated as a major US university, these are still important lessons because these strategies are what will ensure that you have the tools necessary to get yourself recovered quickly, effectively, and under budget.

YOU DON'T DEVELOP ANY STRATEGIES

Disaster-recovery strategies are essentially those that give you potential actions to recover personal function (physical, mental, social, etc.). So, for instance, if you need access to water and you lose it in a disaster, and no bottled water is available, there are a few potential options: the local lake and public water fountains (okay, these are not great strategies, but that only serves to highlight my point). They may not be ideal strategies, but they'll at least provide a temporary solution, depending on the severity of the outage.

The history of disasters has proven that these strategies are essential. In 2021, the *Ever Given* got stuck in the Suez Canal, which is a major shipping pinch point. In 2020 alone, over nineteen thousand ships passed through the canal. The *Ever Given*, a massive 20,000 TEU (the units used to evaluate ship size) ship, took weeks to extricate, as authorities had to work from scratch as shipping clogged, creating massive disruptions around the world.

What happened in the Suez is a perfect illustration that once you have determined the elements of your recovery, how quickly you must do it, and what you can spend, you must finish the final part of the Recovery Sentence. When we don't develop any strategy options, our recovery becomes limited, and we risk not being able to recover before our end goal.

For example, if you simply assume that your pharmacy is going to be open after a disaster to provide you with essential medicine, that means that you are relying solely on the pharmacy company to reopen on time. You are assuming that it has a disaster-recovery plan, that it has people who will be able to come into the pharmacy, that it will be able access the appropriate scripts, that it will get its information systems back, and that it will have 100 percent supply-chain continuity and the medication you need right when you need it. Those are *a lot* of assumptions. To put it in *Seinfeld* terms, you are hoping the company will have your "fitted hat"—and have it at the exact moment you enter Yankee Stadium.

When we default to whatever is offered by a nonprofit, whenever our therapist is available, whenever the pharmacy happens to open, or whenever FEMA decides to give us a loan, we are suddenly under the control of another agency. Your recovery—you guessed it—becomes dependent on someone else. If they don't have your "fitted hat," then your disaster is going to become that much more unpleasant.

YOU DON'T COMPLETE YOUR RECOVERY

Perhaps one of the biggest issues I see in disaster recovery is that people never seem to complete their own recovery. When I read newspaper articles about disasters that occurred years before, inevitably I read text that says, "The community is still reeling" or "Family X hasn't recovered from the fire, even after all these years."

That's really sad. It's even more sad because it doesn't have to be that way. Eventually, the recovery must end, but the only one who can determine that is you. No one seems to set realistic disaster-recovery goals. It's time for you to be the person who does. Doing so will keep the problems introduced by the disaster from continually reoccurring. Resources are critical, but if not allocated properly, they're a waste of time.

I saw this constant state of limbo in the years after Hurricane Katrina, when I worked in the Governor's Office of Homeland Security, during which people were not able to get on with their lives and had to live in squalid conditions in the infamous FEMA trailers dotted throughout New Orleans. They exacerbated already difficult socioeconomic conditions, and no one was able to move forward.

C3 METHOD SOLUTIONS

Let me tell you a secret: with the right strategy, I can 100 percent recover you after *any disaster* in twenty-four hours. Not 10 percent. Not 50 percent. Not 99 percent. *100 percent.* It doesn't matter if it's a cyberattack; a massive, million-acre wildfire; a destructive tornado; or any other incident. Not a doubt in my mind. Once you take control over your own recovery, there is no reason you can't design any disaster. When you've developed the right strategy that fits your time and cost requirements, you can do it. Creating the right strategies is critical and will lower your dependency on any particular option or agency, increasing your resiliency as a result. Otherwise, you'll be stuck drinking the water from your local lake.

COMMAND – "I CAN EMPOWER MYSELF"

When a disaster ends is 100 percent up to you. But, like we covered before, if you don't set strict start and end dates for your recovery, then your recovery stage will *never* officially start and *never* actually end. Identify the areas of your recovery based on this assumption alone. You must have a termination date for your disaster recovery. Don't let the news media, politicians, celebrities, or other influencers dictate that deadline for you. Letting your recovery stage last too long will turn you into a perpetual victim.

Recovery strategies are what provide you with the options necessary to be effective in meeting your recovery goals. They are what empower you to wrest control back from your disaster recovery because with them, you can determine the right path for yourself and not leave yourself vulnerable to or reliant on other people who may not be as prepared for the disaster as you are. There is no such thing as "the only option." There are always multiple options; it is just up to you to figure out what they are.

You're now empowered with the mindset to complete your recovery scenario.

COMMUNICATE – "I CAN EMPOWER OTHERS"

Speak with your team and determine if you are on track with your selected strategies. Many times, these strategies seem great on paper, but when attempted, do not work as first considered. Use the information you gather during the Communication stage to make any necessary adjustments to those strategies. You have to do this if you want them to be effective. While a recovery isn't a straight line, it does require a beginning, a middle, and an end. You need your team to advise you on these stages. Defining strategies might be necessary.

Make calls. Verify your information. Confirm that you have the right information to move forward. Do *not* make any decisions until you have full information on each strategy. Do not make any quick decisions without fully Communicating. Remember also to stay within the timeframe you've established for your recovery—in our example scenario, seven days.

CARRY OUT – "WE CAN EMPOWER EACH OTHER"

PART THREE OF OUR SENTENCE

We now arrive at the final part of the Recovery Sentence. In our example scenario, we started with a blank slate, and now, through an examination of your personal needs, we have come up with this:

- "To recover my physical health, _____ must provide access to my medicine (or a pharmacy) in two days and cost $200."
- "To recover my mental health, _____ must provide access to licensed therapy in seven days and cost $400."
- "To recover my professional health, _____ must provide access to high-speed internet in two days and cost $100."

Now we must figure out what our options are for meeting the requirements we've set. Let's consider the strategies.

WHAT IS THE STRATEGY?

Develop the strategy. Brainstorm any ideas. It doesn't matter what they are; just add them in there. The best way to begin is by talking about the strategies in advance and by not self-editing. Sometimes even the ideas that seem silly at first actually make a lot of sense. For instance, I once worked with a large company in Ohio that had offices throughout the region, and we were trying to develop a backup strategy for its email system. We considered various applications and eventually decided that we would use the courtesy email accounts its website host had provided and were normally not used by anyone. So instead of spending lots of money on new accounts, the company chose to set up those free accounts.

I lay out lots of different strategies with all my clients. Let's explore a few to get you started. Not all of the strategies are perfect—they all have their different ups and downs—but you can at least get a sense of the expectations for each one.

One strategy I get asked about a lot is that of the government. The government does provide some free services during a disaster, and if they are available, I want you to take advantage of them. When I was a kid, after dinner I would ask my mom for ice cream. No matter how much of my dinner I ate, I always wanted to have ice cream. Finally, my mom started telling me that dessert is supposed to be an optional part of a meal. I want you to treat the government, aid agencies, and all external assistance just like ice cream: *nice but not necessary*. If there are free resources available, use them—they can be a tremendous benefit. But do not be fully dependent on them! You will only be disappointed. If they help you, great. But if they don't, it's no big deal. If you approach them in this way, you will still get to make all the decisions. List these resources as an option in your recovery table, but not near the top.

In our example scenario, we've decided to focus on your mental health first. You did some research, and, after considering your options, you've determined that there are eight strategies you can use. You don't have to complete a table like on the next page, but I've provided it to help us as a reference.

This may seem like a lot, but we can pretty quickly narrow things down. We now have to evaluate the effectiveness of each in providing us what we need, checking whether each strategy meets the following requirements of time and cost:

- It must provide us access to a *licensed* therapist
- It must provide it in seven days
- It must cost less than $100 per week

We eliminated Therapist A because they didn't meet our budget. Therapist C can't see us for two weeks, so they don't meet our time requirements. We also eliminated Community Agency A because they don't provide us with a licensed therapist. But there's another possibility. There's a place for government in your recovery, and I am going to show you where that is—in essence, the government can play an important role acting as a last-resort option. The government sometimes provides basic therapy through a disaster-response team. These teams are

Access to Therapy Seven days			
What is the strategy?	How long will it take to start?	How much will it cost?	Is this a licensed therapist?
Therapist A	Four weeks	$150/week	Yes
Therapist B	**One week**	**$20 deducible**	**Yes**
Therapist C	Two weeks	$200/week	Yes
Current therapist	**Immediately**	**$50 deducible**	**Yes**
Mobile app	**Thirty minutes**	**$2,000/six months**	**Yes**
Community Agency A	One hour	$30/week	No
Community Agency B	**Four days**	**$80/week**	**Yes**
Disaster-response team therapist	**Three days**	**Nothing**	**Yes**

not deployed in every disaster; however, when they are, they are available free of charge. Still, do *not* list them as your main option. Use them only as a last-ditch, final option because there will be circumstances when the government and these teams will not be around. Additionally, in any circumstance, government-provided therapy is only going to be *temporary*. In our table, I've listed this option at the bottom for a reason. It's the mental-health equivalent of an EMT.

Remember, these strategies are not meant to be permanent solutions. They are just something to give you access to what you need to get your life back to normal. That's what this initial recovery stage is all about.

Now we must complete the Recovery Sentence by selecting a strategy.

HOW LONG DOES IT TAKE TO START?

Now that we have narrowed our list down from eight to five, let's go through the table, column by column, asking questions as we go. The first question is: How long does the strategy take to start? Determine how long it will take to get your needs met by each option. Remember that the stand-in therapist may not be able to start with you right away. And while a mobile app might have a quick sign-up process, it might not set you up with a therapist right away, either.

We must make sure that our strategies fit the timeline we need. In our example scenario, we've set seven days as the longest you can wait before serious negative consequences occur. Securing a new therapist will probably take a while, since you'll have to find one, get the paperwork started, and set up a session—probably a five- to seven-day process. It's pushing the timeline a bit, but it does line up with our seven-day recovery time. A review of the mobile app's instructions shows that you can get the app and see a therapist within five days. Again, it's a little close, but it does match up with the timeframe.

Remember also that you want to have the right fit with your therapist. Do they have the right philosophy? Will they be able to provide the support you need? Do you even like them? Each of these questions is critical to answer.

HOW DO WE DO IT?

Make sure to consider every step required by a given strategy. In many instances, these steps will impact your timeline for getting your recovery started. For instance, securing a new therapist would require you to search for one, complete their assessment, and schedule a session—and you'd have to factor in the time between each session, too. It's possible that you may not find anything viable in the timeframe that you establish. If that's the case, try to find something temporary. For mental health, that could mean a crisis hotline or any mental-health teams who have been deployed in an emergency.

Access to Therapy Seven days			
What is the strategy?	How long will it take to start?	How much will it cost?	Is this a licensed therapist?
Therapist B	One week	$20 deducible	Yes
Current therapist	Immediately	$50 deducible	Yes
Mobile app	Thirty minutes	$2,000/six months	Yes
Community Agency B	Four days	$80/week	Yes
Disaster-response team therapist	Three days	Nothing	Yes

Now you must select a strategy. And that's what recovery is really about: getting to a place where a temporary solution serves as a bridge to your complete disaster recovery.

FINISH YOUR RECOVERY

Once you have determined all of your strategies for each of the five recovery areas, make your decision and start. Get the tasks done. For instance, your sentence may be "To recover my mental health, I must have access to therapy within seven days and cost me $400 a month." Now that you have selected one of the options, try it out. If it doesn't work out, try another one. That's why it's great to have five. While a given strategy may meet time and cost requirements on paper, the reality is that, for example, a company may not be open when we call or also be shut down as a result of the disaster.

Whatever you decide, the main point is that you'll retain control over the execution of your entire disaster recovery—in each of the areas of your life. And when you have recovered each area, then you will have recovered from the disaster.

Disaster recovery is still largely measured by the number of homes restored, shelters closed, and jobs restarted. But that isn't true recovery. Theoretically, you could be in a shelter with your home destroyed and your family totally separated and still be in total control of a disaster. Or you could be in your $1 million house, totally rebuilt, with your kids back in school—and barely be recovered at all. That is because recovery is built on restoring every element of your life.

What I want to reinforce to you is this: the goal of the recovery in our example scenario *isn't* to get yourself psychologically over the trauma; it's to reach your goal by getting to the therapist within two weeks and at under $400 a month. This will get you to a place where you can then access the resources you need.

For your physical health, we have determined that you must access a pharmacy in two days to get your medication. Let's say you find that Acme Pharmacy has what you need and is able to accept your transfer.

- "To recover my physical health, Acme Pharmacy must provide access to my medication (or a pharmacy) in two days and cost $200."

For your mental health, let's say you decide to select an alternate therapist based on your evaluation:

- "To recover my mental health, Therapist B must provide access to therapy in seven days and cost $200."

If the alternate therapist doesn't work out, you have other options as well. You can still try the mobile app. Maybe your current therapist will recover quickly and be able to fit you into their schedule right away. No matter what, you will meet your requirements to recover your mental health.

But what about your professional health? We can use the same process as before to determine the right strategy. Here is the current sentence:

- "To recover my professional health, _____ must provide access to high-speed internet in two days and cost $100."

Since Aunt Cheryl lives in an area where the internet seems not to have been discovered yet, you have several options. You could go to a café in town that has internet access; you could drive to a nearby city and use your phone as a hotspot; you could even try a public library—anywhere that has the high-speed internet you need. Let's say you decide to go to the local library. It's close and easy to get to—and best of all, it's free. And it's open during the time you'll need it for your corporate meeting.

So here are our final Recovery Sentences:

- "To recover my physical health, Acme Pharmacy must provide access to my medicine (or a pharmacy) in two days and cost $100."
- "To recover my mental health, Therapist B must provide access to licensed therapy in seven days and cost $400 a month."
- "To recover my professional health, the public library must provide access to high-speed internet in two days and cost $100."

There you go. No FEMA. No dealing with the insurance company. No worries about your house. You can focus on those things later when you decide and are able to get back to normal.

As you go through your recovery, keep yourself accountable. Yes, you must consider the long-term elements of your recovery, but getting to a place where you are meeting your basic needs to live and operate is the goal. Keep in mind that you may have to reevaluate your options and strategies as you work through this process.

Ultimately, you must *complete* your recovery. Don't let the doom prevent you from finishing. You may experience a family death, you may see systematic destruction of your community—but you must set that end date. No one is asking you to rush through it. But you must set that date so that you can move forward.

Congratulate yourself for taking a step toward your recovery. Remember, recovery doesn't mean everything is back to normal. It just puts you in a functioning place from which you can later get things back to normal. If you start this recovery process properly, you won't rely on others or assume that they'll handle your recovery for you. In this way, you'll minimize your losses. You can control how you recover—because you have defined the strategies and executed them, within your budget and on your time, not someone else's.

WRAPPING UP: BACK TO SCHOOL

For the employees of CSUN after the earthquake in 1994, recovery was not so simple. They had to determine successful strategies for every element of the university's functioning so that students could return seamlessly to school.

After almost eighteen months of work, they were able to get portable buildings to act as temporary classrooms, and they were able to recover many of the school's administrative functions as well. However, there was one hurdle that remained: they were unable to get to the records room, where student grades and evaluations were located. Since the university was not fully digitized at this point, these hard copy records were the only sources of this important data. After much debate, they attempted various strategies to no avail. They needed those records, but they were stuck in that office. The "red tag" the government had placed on the building made it so that no one could return to get those records until the building was evaluated by a certified structural engineer.

But they left one single strategy as a last-ditch effort. It would be very risky, but if they truly wanted to restore the university, they would need to get those files. So, to grab them out of the cabinets quickly, they did something employees of any modern university would do under the circumstances: they broke into the building and retrieved the records.

Part Five

REVERSE

Transform Disaster into Opportunity
with the C3 Method

Chapter Thirteen

TRANSFORM YOURSELF

On a cold, blustery morning, a young Cambridge University student awoke to the news from a university wall post that classes were cancelled indefinitely and that all students should return home. This was not a total surprise, as it had been common knowledge that a pandemic was raging throughout the United Kingdom and that social distancing was likely going to be the measure implemented by the university. So he quickly gathered his study materials and began the sixty-mile trek home to Lincolnshire.

When he arrived at his farm, he took in the solitude around him and realized that just because the university had closed and social distancing had been implemented, it didn't mean it had to interrupt his research. He was very well known around the school as a brilliant researcher and was very focused on his work. But the weight of classes and student responsibilities had made it very difficult to focus on what he felt were the major projects of his life. So, without any hesitation, and with a pandemic raging around him, he set up his lab and immediately got to work.[62]

The primary reason people become less resilient is because they typically set themselves up to be weaker after a disaster. The inability to return to a normal life and restore family life to the way it was is an economic strain almost without comparison. For people in vulnerable categories, this issue is made even worse. The US Department of Health and Human Services has determined that vulnerable populations are far less likely to be able to recover from disasters than those in mainstream populations.[63]

This results in communities that are less prepared for future disasters and just as likely to face serious consequences from them. *However, it doesn't have to be like this.* In fact, when properly sustained, you can transform any disaster into an opportunity to make your life more resilient to future disasters. I am going to challenge you in these next three chapters to design any disaster in a way that actually reverses its effects and makes you and your community more resilient for the next disaster.

Unfortunately, after a disaster, there are a series of incidents that tend to occur that virtually guarantee that people will miss this valuable opportunity to improve their resilience after an emergency. There are a couple of reasons for this.

YOU DON'T IMPROVE

No matter what disaster you and your community face, you must, at a minimum, seek to learn its lessons. There is always something to learn from it. *Anyone who says their disaster response was perfect is revealing its first flaw.* I told you: 99.97 percent is the best we can do. Much like the drills I described in chapter four, a disaster response has to have its lessons captured and categorized. I see so many people that, after a disaster is over, put everything away and forget about it. Often, this can be the result of the grief process. It's the "acceptance" phase associated with Elisabeth Kübler-Ross's model of grief. Acceptance is often incorrectly associated with forgetting and moving on. This is a major mistake, since the problems that arise from a disaster provide incredibly valuable information that will make you more prepared for next time.

Equipment that didn't work. Supplies that were outdated. Technology that failed. Plans that didn't quite go as . . . well, planned. Insurance companies that were uncooperative. The list goes on and on. But when these lessons aren't captured, the mistakes are *guaranteed* to be repeated. A really good example of this is first-aid kits. In my career, I have seen many decades-old Band-Aids and dried-up antiseptic wipes. The reason for this is simple: people put them away and forget all about them.

When you don't learn from what happened during a disaster, you are sadly doomed to repeat the mistakes next time. Again, there is no disaster response that is ever perfect. Ever. Every disaster response has something to teach us for the next time, and if you are unable to effectively capture those lessons, you'll never get better, and in some instances, you'll get worse. I get that it's hard to admit this; some will not want to revisit their mistakes and will consider them signs of weakness or failure. However, when we decide that we are going to learn from what happened, we take that critical first step in making ourselves more resilient for the next disaster—and through our resiliency, we can remember and honor our loved ones. Recall that in emergency management, we conduct a "hotwash" where we get together as a group after a large incident and discuss the lessons learned. Even professional responders who have seen hundreds of these incidents recognize that there has to be a debriefing to learn how to improve for the next time. Unfortunately, I see far too often that people simply leave these valuable lessons behind.

What results is that people fall into the so-called "preparedness paradox." Described through multiple Harvard University studies, this is a phenomenon in which, after an effective disaster response, one is less incentivized to prepare for future disasters because the lessened severity of the first one made the preparations seem overkill.[64] This will leave you less prepared. This tends to happen with individuals and organizations that have near misses or experience disasters that end up being much smaller than expected. I see this often in areas where a certain disaster is commonplace and people tend to underestimate what is necessary to prepare for larger-scale versions of that disaster. This is a dangerous situation that leads to a complacent, passive mindset.

The mental perspective that tends to dominate disaster response is that of "doom and gloom." Depictions of disasters are essentially universal in focusing on doom and gloom. Media reports highlight the daily death toll of COVID-19; we see families barely surviving a disastrous tornado; others scramble to skirt the maelstrom from a flood in long evacuation lines. Of course, these are all important elements of a disaster to highlight. The problem is that they dominate our perception of disasters so much that it becomes next to impossible to get past the darkness into something that is positive.

Disasters are traumatic incidents. There is no doubt about that. This is especially true if you are dealing with the loss of a loved one or the destruction of your home and possessions. I don't want you to try to artificially suppress that or ignore your emotions. *But you must manage them properly so that they don't paralyze you from improving for the next disaster.*

When we think of disasters, words like "trauma," "death," "utter destruction," and "pandemonium" come to mind. Many times, the implications are that life will be never the same after such incidents. While life may certainly feel like it's never going to be the same, I want you to consider challenging the assumptions that you must, for instance, "get over," "get past," or "accept a loved one's death." Often, these assumptions can make you feel like the world has stopped and that nothing will ever continue because grief will take over and the loss will feel unimaginable.

Well-known researchers of grief have suggested through their models of processing grief that at some point grief ends and that one can start "living" once the acceptance process is complete. They write about letting grief work become personal and recognizing that it is nuanced by culture, meaning, rituals, legacy, and conversation. What this means in practice is that the way you grieve should be highly personalized to you.

I bring this up to encourage you to design your disaster in a way that is meaningful to you, your loved one, your grief, and what you are ready for in processing the disaster. I want to gently encourage you to reconsider waiting until the grief is over before you act; taking sooner action can perhaps be one way of honoring your relationship with your loved one and passing on their legacy. We also cannot honor our loved ones when we don't take control of our grief.

However, when doom and gloom dominate everything and leave no room for something positive, they restrain rational decision-making and strip all hope out of a more resilient tomorrow. People are then less capable of getting their lives back to normal because this makes them increasingly dependent on others to help them get through the disaster. This is the Bystander Effect all over again because the mindset is perpetuated that "If I do nothing, someone else will handle it for me."

When we give up or decide that we're just going to "survive" the disaster, we're handing off responsibility to someone else. It is like we are a bystander in our own life that has surrendered control to others and to the event itself. The goal is to be able to self-regulate your emotions regarding the event and honor your grief, while systemically making yourself more prepared than you were before.

C3 METHOD SOLUTIONS

What I want to do for you in this chapter is to overturn everything you have experienced in disaster recovery and look at the other side of disasters—because once the disaster response is over and you have recovered the basic foundation of your life, it's time to look beyond the darkness of the disaster and examine it differently. I want you to look beyond what the disaster has *destroyed*, and I want you to see what it has *revealed*. The reason I want you to do this is because there are elements of yourself and your community that will be revealed after a disaster has passed. This is the opportunity to learn from it and become more resilient as result.

Of all the changes in mindset I have asked you to make up to this point, this one is by far the biggest. Everyone looks at the negative side of a disaster: all the horrible things that can occur because of these incidents. No one is questioning that; disasters are traumatic incidents, and no one is expecting you to "just get over it." I find it incredibly helpful, however, to use Lorraine Hedtke and John Winslade's model of grief. They suggest the use of "remembering," "re-membering," "rituals," and "legacy." The idea is that you can still honor and celebrate the legacies of your lost loved ones, even though they aren't physically in your life anymore. They can have membership in your life again by being remembered through conversation, legacy, and rituals.

That doesn't mean I want you to deny the disaster or avoid grieving what has been lost. Not at all. Disasters are incredibly traumatic and can have a lasting impact on anyone. However, if you don't identify what your weaknesses were in your disaster response and eliminate them for next time, you are only dooming yourself to larger disasters, more grief, and more loss. This is the time when you have to focus and determine how to make yourself more resilient. Because when you don't, the disaster will continue to disempower you. You are, in essence, letting the disaster dictate how your life is impacted, leaving you to be a bystander in your own disaster response. I'm not claiming that this is going to be easy, especially since we are often trained to view disasters from a single point of perspective. But if you don't want the loss from the previous disaster to be for nothing, you must apply a systematic examination of it. The C3 Method provides you with that framework.

COMMAND – "I CAN EMPOWER MYSELF"

Instead of assuming that a disaster is going to make you weaker, *I want you to see a disaster as a tool to make you a stronger, more resilient person*. It can do that if you let it. Remember, an incident is not really a disaster unless you make it one. If you are able to shift your mindset to a place where the disaster makes you better, you will see it as something you can imminently control.

To do this, you must understand that you are the only one who can prepare yourself for the next disaster. The way to do this is assume *if you don't design the next disaster, then you will waste everything you learned from this one*. I want you to also assume that *you are the only one preparing for the next disaster*. The reason I want you to also make this assumption is because I don't want you to increase your dependence. Don't rely on any other organization to make you better after a disaster. Focus on your own disaster response. This will make you more resilient for next time. Don't squander this opportunity. You can't change the past, so let's focus on the future.

Doom and gloom don't have to dominate how you think. Destruction can be a valuable tool to make you more resilient. In California, the mega wildfires in 2020 had a tremendous effect on the environment: they opened up pinecones that require intense heat to open.[65] As a result, new seeds will be planted, and with proper environmental stewardship, new forests will grow in just a few seasons. This not only slows wildfires but reduces their severity.[66]

As I write this chapter, the drought in California has had a very unique impact on Lake Powell. Environmentalists have long cursed the day Glen Canyon was dammed and the Lake Powell reservoir was formed by flooding the landscape behind it. Thanks to alarmingly low water levels and a two-decades-long drought, that landscape now seems to be returning to its natural state not seen for more than half a century. This means that the habitats there could revert to their original states before humans changed them. Scientists believe that this will restore balance to the ecosystem in that area. This would have never been possible before such a massive drought.

Famed chess grandmaster Garry Kasparov is widely recognized as one of the greatest chess players of all time. He developed a technique where he would sacrifice critical pieces early in the game.[67] His opponents, somewhat confused, would smile at their luck—and just when they thought they would defeat him, Kasparov would turn around and close the trap around their king and force them to resign the game. He saw these seemingly disadvantageous sacrifices as opportunities to develop new strategies and innovative chess positions. He was so successful that his technique is now taught in chess schools around the world. One of the discoveries experts have realized in analyzing his games is that in sacrificing those pieces, Kasparov opened up opportunities that no one had ever seen before.[68] He was able to look at the sacrifices that he would make on the board and say, "Based on those losses, based on my losing those pieces, what strategic error is my opponent going to make now?" When you look at the rubble of a disaster, what opportunity do you see beyond the sacrifice? Disasters can reveal opportunities you would have never otherwise discovered.

One of the effects of the COVID-19 pandemic is that people are now resigning in great numbers. Called the "Great Resignation," many people have simply decided that working in an office, or their career as a whole, isn't for them. There are myriad reasons individuals decided to resign and move on, but one of them is that COVID-19 provided an opportunity to sit at home and evaluate their life: Where are they in life? Are they happy doing what they're doing? Is there something new that they want to try? Do they want to go back to school or work somewhere else? This shift was so dramatic that throughout the start of the pandemic, the *Wall Street Journal* had a column called "Your COVID," which highlighted stories about people who adapted to the changes from the pandemic and improved their lives.[69]

Take what you've gained from your sacrifice and capitalize on it so that you'll be in a stronger position than you were in before. Take the lessons from this disaster and improve things in your life you never had the chance to before. In fact, a disaster may actually help you embrace your job even more. Or it can prompt you to find new work in an industry where there aren't so many vulnerabilities to disasters. Whatever they are, take the lessons from a disaster and move forward with them.

Achieve greater resilience by eliminating situations that make you weak. So, for example, let's say you're working from home for a set amount of days per week, but you know you want something that's a little more action filled. There's many people needed in the healthcare field, so maybe train to be an nurse, a phlebotomist, or an X-ray tech. Those are jobs that are in high demand and have a fair amount of turnover in them, so you could take those jobs if your primary job becomes unavailable.

I love emergency management. I love working with people in preparing them for disasters—but if for some reason I could not do that anymore, I certainly could go back to working in an ambulance again. Look for jobs that are resilient and that put you in a place to be better prepared for disasters.

COMMUNICATE - "I CAN EMPOWER OTHERS"

The first thing we must do is capture the lessons from the disaster. As we've talked about throughout the book, most post-disaster actions disempower you because they help you assume that if you do nothing, someone else will do it for you. However, now you must design your next disaster . . . and any disaster that comes after. The way to do that is to systematically identify weaknesses and convert them into strengths by *asking the right questions* of yourself.

When I first started my company, Hytropy Disaster Management, I decided to design disaster plans in a radically new way. The pages of my plans were split in half: on the left side were the response steps, written in short bullet points, using common non-jargon language. Then, for each step, on the right side there was nothing . . . but an empty box. Clients asked me why I did that, and I told them that this was *their* disaster plan, not mine. And that associated space was for them to tell *me* how to make *their* plan better. For each associated step, that blank box was their opportunity to tell me if that step worked well or if there was a way to improve it for the next disaster. They were experts of their businesses, and it was my job to write a disaster plan that maximized their effectiveness and empowered them best.

When you complete your disaster response, there is a quick and easy way to determine how to get better. Take a sheet of paper and draw vertical lines separating the paper into three parts. The leftmost column will contain a list of disaster-response topics. Then, at the top of the second column, I want you to write the question: "What went well?" Then, on the right, I want you to write, "What can I make better?" This doesn't point to failure or place blame; it's a neutral sentence that doesn't single anyone out. Asking these two questions will help you evaluate what needs to be improved and what you already have working. These questions are about getting better for the future. In many cases, weaknesses will be obvious to you: you could've moved the priceless grandfather clock that was almost destroyed; you had no power and no flashlights; you didn't know how to run the generator.

This last question will force you to think into the future and look at how to prepare better for the next emergency. If possible, write down everything that you've learned. Call people to brainstorm what could have been improved and what could be done differently in the future.

Topic Area	What went well?	What can I make better?
Disaster Plan		
Equipment		
Supplies		
Technology		
Focus		
Scene Assessment		
Scene Safety		
ESIPL		
Incident Stabilization		
Property Triage		
Recovery Identification		
Recovery Time and Cost		
Recovery Strategies		

Complete this table after *every* disaster, big or small. No exceptions. Determine what worked well and what didn't. By completing this, you will have conducted a thorough examination of your disaster process. As you read over it, keep a keen eye out for anything marking dependence.

CARRY OUT - "WE CAN EMPOWER EACH OTHER"

Now that we have discovered the weaknesses in our disaster response, we need to transform them into strengths. Go through the third column, "What can I make better?" and eliminate the weaknesses through new strategies. If equipment didn't work the way it claimed, then it is time to get new equipment. If the evacuation location you wanted to go to wasn't available, then it's time to select a different one. If you weren't able to secure your collection of sports memorabilia, then it's time to make arrangements for their transport if you ever have to evacuate again. This is the stage to *take action*.

Don't wait. Do it now, when the disaster is still fresh. Don't wait too long because you'll get involved in other things and forget to come back to your list.

In this way, you can fully wrest control from the hands of any disaster.

INCREASING YOUR RESILIENCE

Now that we have learned the lessons we needed to, it's time to go a step further. I want you to be very self-focused on the five recovery areas of your life.

Instead of determining what has been destroyed, I want you to look at what's been revealed. This is the heart of what it means to design any disaster. I want you to see things differently. We've already discussed the issues of grieving through a disaster and dealing with the initial recovery. We are now beyond that, recognizing that disasters are inevitable and opportunities to improve from. I want you to see your life through a different lens.

For each of the following areas, ask one question: What's been revealed? Not what's been destroyed, and not what's been lost. I know you can focus on those already. What opportunities to become more resilient have suddenly appeared that would otherwise never have been visible?

- Physical
- Mental
- Social
- Financial
- Professional

By asking these questions, you are forcing yourself to view the disaster through multiple perspectives. What you may find is that the obstacle has actually made you stronger. Perhaps you're more empowered in certain areas of your life because of what you've been through. That disaster may have taken a lot from you, but you're going to be stronger for it. Look at every negative from two sides. You might have discovered that your insurance company sucks.

Good. Time to find a new one that better suits your needs. Becoming empowered to make changes will make you more resilient. You will transform your life the way you want to. You will control your disasters; they will no longer control you.

Any disaster may afford you the opportunity to become stronger. You don't want to miss a golden opportunity to change your life for the better, so be fully in Command of your own disaster. Capitalize on it. You might find that what was destroyed yielded some good. Take advantage of opportunities to do the things you've been wanting to do for years. No matter what the disaster, no matter how small, there is something that you can get out of the five recovery areas post-disaster that will make you stronger than you were before.

PHYSICAL

Examine how the disaster affected you physically. Maybe you realized that you live in an area that's way too fire prone, or maybe the government didn't do a good job of warning you. Perhaps the evacuation location was terrible or too dangerous.

But I want you to look at your life as a whole and see how it can be improved. In a lighter example, one of the major life adjustments I had to make during the COVID-19 pandemic was that I had to stay home from the gym for nearly a year. I'm a gym rat, so it was driving me crazy because working out is a major stress reliever for me. So what I did was purchase and place gym equipment in my garage. And while the gym has now reopened, I've since discovered that there are certain kinds of workouts I enjoy doing at home better. I was able to transform my workouts as well.

MENTAL

Perhaps you found that you were unable to cope with the emotions related to the disaster. Often, disasters bring up unhealthy coping behaviors that were used to survive while growing up; they force us to confront them again to see if they will still be useful. The COVID-19 pandemic deeply challenged people's feelings regarding isolation, grief, and relationships. Families were forced to spend more time with each other in lockdown, and the number of those relying on alcohol and substances to cope skyrocketed, as well as reports of abuse, discoveries of affairs, and people dying of COVID-19. If you need to get a therapist, do that, or find another type of emotional support that makes space for your grief and is supportive of designing your disaster.

SOCIAL

Disaster recovery isn't just about immediate physical or mental health. It may be that a disaster will expose something important to you. Maybe you've always wanted to get a pet, be closer to your family, find a religious institution to affiliate with, help people in a new career field, become debt-free, or volunteer for a nonprofit. If a disaster provides an opportunity to do one of these things, whatever it is, do it. Don't wait, or you will lose the momentum.

FINANCIAL

I once had my personal laptop destroyed during a disaster, and I was very angry that I hadn't been able to back up a few documents—but then I realized something: I hated that laptop. It was slow. It was not particularly user-friendly. And it periodically overheated when I traveled. So I got a new laptop that I like so much more. With it, I was able to start doing livestreams on disaster preparedness and enhance my social-media presence and the videos I had been creating.

PROFESSIONAL

Finally, let's talk about our professional or educational lives. There is no limit to the changes you can make to yourself professionally or educationally. I once had a client who owned an Italian restaurant in the California Wine Country. When I was writing her recovery plan, I asked her a question I pose to all my clients: If you experience a disaster and your business is destroyed, will you want to recover? She was shocked. She asked me what I meant by that. If the restaurant were to be destroyed by an earthquake or burned in a wildfire conflagration, I asked, would she want to rebuild? She hesitated and asked what would happen if she said no. I told her I would write in her business continuity plan that she would cash the insurance check and walk away. She said she would give it some thought.

About a month later, she called me and told me that if the restaurant were to be destroyed, she would take the insurance money and live and work in a restaurant overseas. So when I finished her plan, I sent it to her, and the last line of the recovery plan read, "If restaurant is destroyed, owner plans not to recover." All I asked her to do was to Communicate this information to her employees, who deserved to know and might have to look for new jobs in case of a disaster. So now if the restaurant is destroyed, the owner has a way out. That's her way of turning a disaster into an opportunity for herself.

In 2002, the Disaster Recovery Institute International completed a study of the disaster recovery after the 1993 World Trade Center bombing. It examined the recovery times of every business that had been affected by the terrorist attack and then compared them to the number of companies still in business after five years. The results were astonishing: if a company hadn't recovered in fourteen days, it only had a 20 percent chance of still being in business after five years.[70] In other words, preparing properly for disasters and recovering quickly from them will make you more resilient.

You are in Command of your own disaster. Now that you have determined all this, you can better evaluate your options. I'm not advocating for you to quit your job or do something drastic. But you can do something that will turn the disaster into an incredible opportunity for you. By doing so, you will take ownership over the aftermath of any disaster. It starts by asking those three questions: What's been destroyed, what's been revealed, and what am I going to do about it? Disasters can be opportunities that you may never get again.

Once you have finished your own recovery, you can help others with theirs. You can make the difference that larger bureaucratic organizations struggle to make. This, in essence, empowers the next person. You can do this for your family, your colleagues, or even a vulnerable person. That will be the focus of the next chapter: the way to design any disaster for your community.

WRAPPING UP: FINDING FREEDOM (AND GRAVITY) ON THE FARM

You must understand that you are the only one who can prepare yourself for the next disaster. The way to do this is to assume that *if you don't design the next disaster, you will waste everything you learned in this one.*

Disasters, whether a hurricane, earthquake, or volcanic eruption, can harness your best self and provide you with new opportunities large and small . . .

if you are willing to change your mindset from not just seeing what the disaster has destroyed but also what it has revealed. This change in worldview can make a major difference in what you can accomplish, and you might just amaze yourself with what is revealed to you, even on a farm in Lincolnshire.

That Cambridge student continued to work throughout the plague uninterrupted, using the solitude to give him the momentum he needed to make breakthroughs in optics, motion, and gravity. He didn't allow the raging pandemic to keep him from his life's work. In fact, the additional time it gave him provided the freedom and intellectual flexibility to work day and night on the most difficult intellectual challenges of his age, including the invention of calculus. In fact, twenty years later, that scholar was asked to reflect upon what he had accomplished during his time away from the university during the pandemic. He said, "I was in the prime of my age for invention & minded Mathematics & Philosophy more than at any time since."[71]

The pandemic he was referring to wasn't in 2020, and it wasn't the COVID-19 pandemic. The year was 1665. And the scholar's name was Sir Isaac Newton.

Chapter Fourteen

TRANSFORM YOUR COMMUNITY

I n the days after the 1906 earthquake in San Francisco, California, a lone
banker stood outside the damaged façade of his broken bank. His name was
Amadeo Pietro Giannini, and he was an Italian immigrant who had opened
his little Bank of Italy in the Bay Area of California. While his was only a minor
city bank, the day after the earthquake, seeing the damage it had caused the
city and the suffering to its people, Giannini decided to do something extraor-
dinary. With two of his employees, he entered the ruined structure of the bank
and opened the safe. He then put out a table in front of his bank, pulled out
a ledger book, and issued loans to any person who requested them. He didn't
require identification or any other traditional verification method. He offered
them through a handshake.[72]

Most disaster books end here. Now that we have discussed how to ready
yourself for, react to, respond to, and recover from a disaster, there doesn't seem
to be a need to do more. However, I want to challenge your thinking about
disasters entirely. I want you to look beyond the destruction of a disaster and
see how you can make your life better afterward. Now, again, I'm not trying to
be a doe-eyed Pollyanna who is endlessly optimistic—because disasters can be
devastating. But I don't want you to become a victim of your circumstances.
You are stronger than that, and you can be even better after the disaster has
passed. You just have to make some adjustments in your thinking, much like

Giannini did after the San Francisco earthquake. He knew he could make a major difference in people's lives by doing something as minor as issuing loans with only a handshake.

I strongly believe that disasters can make not just you but your entire community stronger and more resilient.

COMMUNITIES ARE LESS RESILIENT AFTER A DISASTER

It's amazing to me that communities can be left worse off and less resilient even after billions of dollars are spent—when the reality is that a disaster can make you more resilient and can help minimize the impacts of the next one.

For example, small businesses, which I have devoted much of my professional career to assisting, are sometimes rendered so weak after a disaster that they never come back. Ninety-four percent of companies suffering from a catastrophic data loss do not survive—43 percent never reopen and 51 percent close within two years.[73]

I consider small-business owners to be generally vulnerable because they are always on a precipice. Most businesses in the United States are small, but almost 98 percent of all businesses are what we characterize as microbusinesses with five or fewer employees. Given that their profit margins tend to be razor-thin, they are incredibly vulnerable to even minor shocks in infrastructure systems. Without access to equity markets and sophisticated recovery schemes, they are likely to fail during any disaster. Nonprofit statistics are little better.

After Hurricane Katrina, I saw many small businesses that tried to reopen, but within a year or two, they were gone. Many collapsed because they were artificially propped up by disaster money that didn't truly give them what they need: a process of recovery. It is beyond the scope of this book to apply the C3 Method to small businesses, but as someone who has written more small-business disaster plans than perhaps any other human being who has ever lived, I have a strong sense of what will happen when a small business doesn't prepare for disasters.

Like small businesses, people who are in vulnerable populations of various types tend to be disproportionately impacted by disasters—and that would make sense because they don't have access to equity markets and to public financing that others might. Vulnerable people and their businesses are likely to deal with significant financial strain or go out of business altogether.

Disaster-response and recovery organizations, while well meaning, many times make it more difficult for small businesses to recover. When you give things out for free, small businesses often suffer as purchasing goes down. This harms their recovery. This actually happened in Haiti in 2010: when global aid organizations started importing tons of food, local farmers and local markets went entirely out of business. When you take Command, you should do so in a way that makes sense for what's going on in your community. Taking Command is going to look a little different in every disaster.

These kinds of impacts are not limited to small businesses. Schools (both public and private) can also be disproportionally affected. For instance, many schools after the 2011 tornado in Joplin, Missouri, still had visible operational disruption even by 2013. Loss of records, equipment, and critical technology prevented them from getting into a state of critical recovery.

Other institutions important to your community may not recover, either. Many people simply assume that everything will work out naturally and that organizations will right themselves quickly. Depending on the disaster, this can be a dangerous misconception. And as individuals remain weak, the community will be deeply affected.

The usual solution that is thrown at this problem is money. However, money is not a guarantee for community recovery. First, any disaster that involves the exchange of money is a magnet for all kinds of criminals and con artists. Every disaster is used by criminals to steal donations from the communities that money is meant to support. Throughout the COVID-19 pandemic, criminals managed over two dozen fake nonprofit funds, collecting millions of dollars that were supposed to be sent to vulnerable communities most impacted by the pandemic.

Theft has gotten so bad that the US Department of Justice in 2005 set up an agency called the National Center for Disaster Fraud, which investigates scams and cons perpetuated during disasters. In the aftermath of Hurricane Katrina, more than 6,400 campaigns on the crowdfunding site GoFundMe were determined to be scams. After every major disaster, there are reports of hundreds of similar charity scams. When you randomly participate in them, you are doing what we call "drive-by philanthropy," which means that you aren't taking Command of your money. You're simply contributing to causes so you can feel like you're making a difference, when you may not actually be doing so because you don't know where the money is directly going.

Putting money into random charities is not effective. That money gets wasted with mass inefficiency and corruption and it doesn't help anyone. Participating in community recovery in this way relies on others to handle your money for you. When you do this, you hand control of the disaster over to someone else who doesn't know your community and to an organization that may not truly care about assisting your community's recovery. For example, after the COVID-19 pandemic was declared by the World Health Organization in March of 2020,[74] fraudulent nonprofits and scammers did everything possible to steal millions of dollars of aid. In addition, some large corporations took advantage of Paycheck Protection Program loans that were meant for independent small businesses not under a corporate umbrella. Few returned the money.[75]

Government inefficiency and waste is just as prevalent. Stories about wasted or stolen FEMA and SBA money is always present in every major disaster. When this occurs, a community can remain in a perpetual state of not recovering.

It doesn't just have to be criminal activity or government waste that erodes the effectiveness of disaster funds. Resource limitations also restrain the ability of a community to rebound. Community institutions do their best to distribute funds appropriately, but their resources can be stretched to the limit, like they were in the 2017 Atlantic hurricane season. Vulnerable communities feel the brunt of these effects. Community traumas, particularly those of large-scale natural disasters, disproportionally impact these vulnerable groups.

Money cannot easily solve the problems created by disasters because many communities are also unable to recover as a result of community trauma and devastation. Many communities get so traumatized from a disaster that they are never able to truly collect themselves. I don't take the loss of businesses and lives in communities lightly. When human lives are lost, the effect on individuals and communities can last for a very long time. There's collective grief and community trauma in addition to individual grief. Consider that Hurricane Katrina happened almost eighteen years ago—and many in that community are still processing their collective grief and trauma. In addition, terrorist attacks accompanied by the deployment of a weapon of mass destruction, like a chemical or nuclear weapon, can fundamentally change the character of a community forever.

The issue is that institutions often do not provide long-term solutions to these kinds of disasters. They offer quick support and then leave. As a result, a community's recovery never finishes. This produces lower economic and social activity: a city in decline.

I have no problem with a community receiving help from outside. In fact, I encourage it. But the problem lies in when communities create a long-term dependency on outside organizations because the internal incentive to improve is eliminated by their support. This, then, reinforces the Bystander Effect.

C3 METHOD SOLUTIONS

I want to propose a unique way to work with your community. If you use the C3 Method to transform your community, you can design any disaster. What I want to do is turn you into a Giannini. Create sustainability, not a quick jolt. Giannini offered loans, not grants. He didn't want people to become dependent. He wanted them to build wealth. I want everything you do to create a situation of greater sustainability and greater ability for organizations in your community to be resilient against future disasters. You can do this with the C3 Method.

COMMAND - "I CAN EMPOWER MYSELF"

"If I do nothing, no one else will, either"—embrace that mindset, and you will be able to empower yourself. This was Giannini's idea. Assume that the disaster is an opportunity to make your community stronger and more resilient. Assume that *if you don't recover your community, no one else will, either.* Stop expecting outside forces or agencies to do it for you. They can't and won't. You're now empowered with the mindset that you can design any disaster on your own.

I want to propose to you a brand-new framework of helping those around you get stronger. I want you to target a specific organization that you want to assist in a disaster and help organize its recovery. Be highly targeted by organizing a team of individuals to focus on one person's recovery with financial, logistical, and other support. To address community grief and collective trauma, a systemic approach of a compilation of disaster teams, mental-health professionals, community members, educators, and first responders will be helpful. But this will require many people. I'm not expecting you to wage a one-person war on trauma. Put together a team that can address it within your sphere of influence.

Take Command of your money, resources, and time before you donate them. If you want to make a truly sustainable donation, you have to ensure that your money is going to something that will benefit the community, not make it more dependent on outside people or organizations.

I would like you to start with people who you know, so consider beginning with someone in your family. There may be someone who has been directly impacted by the disaster. You should form a team and work directly with that person, using the recovery table that I showed you earlier in chapter twelve. Determine what they need to recover, whether it is physical, mental, financial, or spiritual.

COMMUNICATE - "I CAN EMPOWER OTHERS"
Establish a team of people that will work with you. This group will determine the best ways to contribute to a particular organization. Keep in mind that your team members don't all have to be physically in the same place.

CARRY OUT - "WE CAN EMPOWER EACH OTHER"
In the wake of any disaster, there is always an element of community where people really want to be able to help their neighbors, their businesses, and their friends. The best way to do that is through applying the C3 Method to every part of a community. Volunteering and getting involved in nonprofit causes—and doing whatever else is possible after a disaster—has characterized emergency management in the United States and elsewhere for a very long time. However, I want you to do more. You can participate in a myriad of ways, and you and your team don't even have to be part of the affected community.

Nonprofits
You can obviously give money. You won't be giving out loans, but you can still retain full Command of your money by deciding where it will go and by Communicating your expectations to the nonprofits you donate to. Provide complete instructions as to how the money should be spent. This is called "direct

giving" and is an important counter to drive-by philanthropy. This allows you to decrease your dependency on others, retain full control over your money, and maximize the benefits of your giving.

When I was a shelter manager for the American Red Cross, I found out that if people allocated their donations to a specific shelter, the Red Cross faced legal consequences if that money ended up not going to the right place. I even verified this with an attorney. That year, I was able to more effectively garner support for the shelter I was running, and we were able to support its community and get it the aid it needed.

The other obvious way to give to nonprofits is by volunteering your time. Since becoming a professional emergency manager, I have volunteered in my spare time during disasters to nonprofits focused on evacuated peoples and animals, and I've helped design policies and procedures for them as well. I have been a Community Emergency Response Team member for a long time, and it is something I highly recommend, as it provides some of the most basic disaster skills.

Small Businesses

You can make a major difference in a small business. The way to do this is by investing in it. There are many creative avenues to jolt sustainable growth for a small business after a major disaster. For instance, a recent phenomenon in recent years is the "cash mob," which seeks to give a quick injection of funds to small businesses. I organized one of these for a company affected by a tornado. I called it the Disaster Cash Mob, and it had immediate results. During the COVID-19 pandemic, Domino's Pizza purchased gift cards from small restaurants in their areas to give them a boost. This is something that can be quickly organized that is more than just simply giving a business free money.[76] You want to ensure that small businesses can get back to operation as quickly as possible, which will lower their dependency on the government or other organizations to do that for them. This will incentivize them to provide you with a future product or service, even if they aren't able to do so at that moment because of the disaster interruption. This then creates long-term sustainability for small businesses. These may seem like subtle and small actions, but the growth and sustainability of a small business's economy after a disaster can come down to very small incentives.

Communities at Large

There is a lot you can do for your community at large. You must encourage your local government to completely improve the landscape. For instance, during the Iowa flood in 2008, ten square miles of Cedar Rapids were left underwater. That was 14 percent of the city. Seeing an opportunity to revive a blighted community, the city worked with local businesses to use $1 billion in funds from the government. With those funds, they not only revived the city but also created sustained business for companies operating directly in the community, generating local wealth that would otherwise need to be provided by the government.

WRAPPING UP: DREAMS FROM DISASTER

Don't let a disaster point you in the direction that your life (or the life of your community) needs to go or tell you what needs to stay the same. That doesn't need to happen. Instead, look at the disaster and ask, "How can this make us better than we ever were before?"

You're going to find that there is so much more to your life than just the disaster itself, and you're going to discover ways in which you can improve your life and improve those around you, much like Giannini did when his small Bank of Italy was destroyed.

After the earthquake, Giannini decided that he wasn't going to replace the original sign he'd hung above his bank. He decided that this was a chance to turn his bank into something much larger. So, just a few weeks later, he put up a new sign above his business. We would certainly recognize it today. We now know it as Bank of America.

Chapter Fifteen

DESIGN THE NEXT DISASTER

In Indonesia's island of Java, there lives a group of people in the village of Balerante. These people live a simple existence in the shadow of Mount Merapi, one of the most active volcanoes in Indonesia. In fact, it has erupted more than eighty-two times since the sixteenth century, with an eruption cycle every two to seven years. In October and November of 2010, Mount Merapi experienced its largest eruption since 1870, violently spewing lava, launching rocks into the air, belching toxic gases, sparking landslides, and raining down ash upon the village below.

Trying to be proactive in the years after the eruption, the local government made the relocation of the villagers to a safer, less threatened area a high priority. The risk of the volcano erupting again was omnipresent. However, the villagers shocked government officials when they refused to leave Mt. Merapi, explaining that they had tied their livelihoods (with the rich farmland that resulted from the volcanic dust), their culture, and their society to the volcano and the area around it. When the government asked why they would remain in an area with such a high volcanic risk, they replied that they didn't mind because they were "living in harmony with disaster." They had lived with the volcano for a long time and not only understood it but had also tied their entire society to its fate.

While the government was doing what it thought was best for them, the villagers with their simple lifestyle were trying to teach it something that even the most modern twenty-first century country can many times forget: you can't prevent disasters from happening. But you can try to live your life in a way that harmonizes with them and empowers you to be resilient as a result.

That's the same message I want to now translate to you: you can thrive in the Age of Disasters if you know how to think about them, accepting what they are, what they aren't, and tying your life to them in a way that harmonizes your physical, mental, spiritual, financial, and professional health with the disasters you face.

PEOPLE FIGHT DISASTERS

Today, people continue to fight the disasters in their communities. They do everything they can but don't realize that, much like the "earthquake" in the Studio Tour at Universal Studios, they are going to happen anyway. There is way too much pessimism surrounding disasters, and most people do not have a healthy relationship toward what a disaster really represents: an opportunity to be more resilient for the next one.

Psychologically, this can result in losing perspective because doom and gloom can overwhelm you. We are now in an age where there are countless global challenges to face—not only climate change but also serious threats to our digital infrastructure, and even inflation, which erodes our purchasing power. The problem is, the more you try to fight disasters, the more you will exhaust yourself because you simply can't defeat disasters. They don't work like that.

C3 METHOD SOLUTIONS

COMMAND - "I CAN EMPOWER MYSELF"

No matter how tech-savvy you are, where you live, or what you do, I want you to become just like those Indonesian villagers. I want you to make one last assumption, no matter the scope of what's been lost. *I want you to assume that the beauty and destruction of disasters are exactly the same.* I want you to live your life by treating disasters exactly the way I said you should in the introduction to this book: as a part of your community. This is the key to the Indonesian villagers' philosophy.

First, you need a recognition that disasters are going to occur. You can't stop them. So don't fight them. Facing disaster is a part of living somewhere that matters to you. I remember my first day in Louisiana; it was August when I arrived, and it was more humid than any time I could ever imagine. Hot as an oven. But that's just part of living in Louisiana.

If you choose to live somewhere where there is a greater likelihood of wildfire, then either embrace it or move. If you decide to stay, then just accept that you are going to have a higher probability of a wildfire and prepare yourself around this choice.

I am very careful about what I eat, but when I have my weekly cheat meal, I am very much an ice-cream person. Now, I know I'm not supposed to eat ice cream very much, as I work out regularly and am a recreational athlete. So I used to beat myself up about it and get so angry whenver I would succumb to eating ice cream. I made myself completely miserable. Then I realized: that mindset was ruining my ice-cream experience. So I changed the way I thought about ice cream. I now have the attitude that if I eat ice cream, great! I should enjoy it. That's the purpose of ice cream. But I have to accept that if I do so, I will have to work out more the next day.

Have an identical attitude toward disasters. If you decide to live near the beautiful beaches in Florida (you eat the ice cream), you're going to have storms with 134-miles-per-hour winds from time to time (you'll have to work out more to compensate). If you don't want to accept that, then you can't live there. If you live in San Francisco, the earth is going to shake periodically. If you live in Oregon, there are going to be days where the air is smoky from periodic wild fires. But don't let these things destroy what you enjoy about your community.

Occasionally, I read silly news stories about places that have no disasters. I'm telling you, that's a fairy tale, like the mystical hand sanitizer that kills 100 percent of bacteria and germs. Disasters are inevitable and a unique part of your community, so learn to coexist with them. But that doesn't mean you have to let them burn your house down or destroy your beloved photo albums. That is why the C3 Method is so valuable; as you've seen, it gives you a framework for negotiating with disasters. Now all you need is to live in harmony with them.

COMMUNICATE - "I CAN EMPOWER OTHERS"

I want your team to be anyone in the world. This time, I don't want you to restrict yourself. Demonstrate how well you live in harmony with disasters by your example. Focus yourself, your community, your government, your business, your school, and your family by encouraging them to take Command over every respect of the disaster. That is how you will live in harmony with it—with a focused, measured approach via the C3 Method.

CARRY OUT - "WE CAN EMPOWER EACH OTHER"

I told you in the introduction to this book that true disaster preparedness is not a linear, unidirectional activity. You have discovered that it's a cycle, with every step feeding into the next. You should codify this philosophy in everything you do.

The nineteenth-century philosopher Henry David Thoreau used a key metaphor to help people understand how to view things differently. He used to contort himself into various poses and look at the same landscape from every conceivable angle. He would look straight on, from the side, from between his legs, and after climbing up a tree. What he was trying to demonstrate was that a landscape remains the same; it is only our perception toward it that makes the difference.

This is what will help us see through the darkness. When we look at the destruction that a disaster has caused to our landscape, Thoreau counsels us to see "every storm and every drop in it [as] a rainbow."[77]

WRAPPING UP: FINDING YOUR RIGHT NUMBER

It is your mindset that will help you live in the world of disasters. The villagers in Indonesia don't have smartphones, red backpacks, or a sophisticated emergency-management infrastructure.[78] But they have the right mindset needed to live in this Age of Disasters.

In the end, it's up to you. I hope this book has helped you see that disasters don't have to be doom and gloom. I want to impart my enthusiasm for disaster preparedness and show you what I have learned from being an emergency manager: that you can truly *Command, Communicate,* and *Carry Out* any disaster response. I love helping people, and I hope I was able to help you, too.

Disasters are going to continue no matter what we do, whether it is a swarm of locusts, a massive cyberattack, a shooting, a tsunami, or the little green men have invaded. We can't control that. What we can control is our response to them. Just remember, whether you're facing a Category 5 hurricane, an 8.0 earthquake, a EF5 tornado, a collapsing bridge, or a catastrophic terrorist attack, you can overcome it, and you can make yourself stronger, more resilient, and readier to address the disasters of the future.

When you truly embrace the C3 Method and take the actions that I have described in this book, from disaster planning, training, and drills, to reacting and evacuating, to recovering and reversing disaster, you will never be a disaster victim ever again. You will be able to take Command, Communicate, and Carry-Out in the face of any incident—and *Design Any Disaster.*

ACKNOWLEDGMENTS

Writing a book is one of those crucibles in life that takes a lot but gives back so much more. To do it successfully requires the support of so many people.

I am first eternally grateful to the Benbella Books team. They each generously gave of their time working with a new author to make this book successful. Leah Wilson, my incredible acquiring editor, without whom this book would not have been realistically possible, was willing to accept my many last-second revisions, was an unbelievable tour guide in this journey, and did it all with great humor. Jennifer Canzoneri, Alicia Kania, Madeline Grigg, Monica Lowry, Sarah Avinger, and many others each provided patient guidance and were an absolute pleasure to work with throughout this process.

A very special thanks to my editor Greg Brown, who, to say the least, was incredibly flexible and reasonable in working with me through the ups and downs of writing. I have discovered the joys and frustrations of writing a cohesive book, and he bore the brunt of my responses to both. I thank him for his time, energy, and insights as I developed this work.

I would also like to offer a special thanks to Jonathan Adams for tirelessly working with me during the early stages of this book to meld it into an organized, thoughtful narrative. He listened to all of my many presentations and patiently demonstrated how to convert them into a written book.

Thank you to my terrific agents, Steve Troha and Jamie Chambliss at Folio. I couldn't have asked for better representation. Also, thank you to my book consultant, Lindi Stoller, who was the first one to see the potential of this project during the height of the pandemic.

My gratitude to the entire Hytropy Disaster Management and Disaster Hawk® teams; I am honored to serve as their CEO. They are an incredible group of people who are constantly inventing ways to support our small business and family clients before, during, and after disasters. I especially want to thank my VP of Customer Service, Michelle Cavanaugh, who helped pick up the slack when I was sequestered in my office drafting and redrafting this book.

We all have to start somewhere. I also owe thanks to Susan Severance, the greatest boss I ever had in emergency preparedness. She took a young man with huge ideas but a small resume and put him on the path to becoming a successful emergency manager. Her mentorship and friendship are things I will cherish throughout my life.

My family, who I am so grateful to have in my life, are the one constant as I pursue this grand, if unconventional adventure of life. My father is the best business continuity planner and the greatest role model I could ask for. He provided me the life skills both professionally and personally that have turned me into the man I am today. My mother has given me immeasurable love and a huge loan of support that I don't think I will ever be able to repay. My grandmother and brother live far away but are very close to my heart.

My biggest thanks to my significant other. I can't describe in words what a positive presence she is in my life. She patiently reads drafts, makes sure I am fed when I have skipped a meal or two while I am working, and helps keep me sane while I juggle the responsibilities of life. She does all of this with the patience of a saint.

Finally, to all others who helped get me here—my friends, my colleagues, clients, and other family members who gave themselves to support me: thank you.

NOTES

1   Smith, Adam B. 2021. "2020 U.S. Billion-Dollar Weather and Climate Disasters in Historical Context." Climate.Gov. https://www.climate.gov/disasters2020.

2   NASA. 2020. "California's August Complex Largest Fire in State's History." National Aeronautics and Space Administration.

3   Ibid.

4   Baskar, Pranav. 2022. "Locusts Are a Plague of Biblical Scope in 2020. Why? And . . . What Are They Exactly?" *NPR*. https://www.npr.org/sections/goatsandsoda/2020/06/14 /876002404/locusts-are-a-plague-of-biblical-scope-in-2020-why-and-what-are-they-exactly.

5   Ibid.

6   D. LaVanchy, G. Thomas, Michael W. Kerwin, and James K. Adamson. 2019. "Beyond 'Day Zero': Insights and Lessons from Cape Town (South Africa)." *Hydrogeology Journal* 27 (5): 1537–1540. doi:10.1007/s10040-019-01979-0.

7   Taylor, Brian, and Martin Wachs. 2022. "Carmageddon in Los Angeles: The Sizzle and The Fizzle." *ACCESS* Magazine. https://www.accessmagazine.org/spring-2014/carmageddon -los-angeles-sizzle-fizzle/.

8   Schildkraut, Jaclyn, and H. Jaymi Elsass. *Mass Shootings: Media, Myths, and Realities: Media, Myths, and Realities.* ABC-CLIO, 2016.

9   Duncan, T. Stanley. "Death in the Office: Workplace Homicides." FBI L. Enforcement Bull. 64 (1995): 20.

10 Wichaidit, Wit. 2022. "Current Knowledge on Potential Determinants of Mass Public Shooting Perpetration and Casualties: A Systematic Review." doi:10.1101/2022.06.30.222 77119.

11 "Costa Rica's New President Faces Immediate Challenges." 2022. Emerald Expert Briefings. doi:10.1108/oxan-db270270.

12 Alexander, Meredith, Ashley Chase, Kelly Chase, and James S. O'Rourke. "Sony Pictures Entertainment, Inc.: A Cybersecurity Attack from North Korea (A)." *SAGE Business Cases.* London: SAGE Publications Ltd., 2022. https://dx.doi.org/10.4135/9781526403087.

13   "Jump In Cyber Attacks During Covid-19 Confinement." 2020. *SWI.* https://www. swissinfo.ch/eng/sci-tech/jump-in-cyber-attacks-during-covid-19-confinement/45818794.

14   Smith, Stephanie. "Out of Gas: A Deep Dive into the Colonial Pipeline Cyberattack." *SAGE Business Cases.* London: SAGE Publications Ltd., 2022. https://dx.doi. org/10.4135/9781529605679.

15   Albahar, Marwan. 2017. "Cyber Attacks and Terrorism: A Twenty-First Century Conundrum." *Science and Engineering Ethics* 25 (4): 993-1006. doi:10.1007/s11948-016-9864-0.

16   "Chest Pain: First Aid." 2022. Mayo Clinic. https://www.mayoclinic.org/first-aid/first-aid -chest-pain/basics/art-20056705.

17   Fischer, Peter, Tobias Greitemeyer, Andreas Kastenmüller, Joachim I. Krueger, Claudia Vogrincic, Dieter Frey, Moritz Heene, Magdalena Wicher, and Martina Kainbacher. 2011. "The Bystander-Effect: A Meta-Analytic Review on Bystander Intervention in Dangerous and Non-Dangerous Emergencies." *Psychological Bulletin* 137 (4): 517–37. doi:10.1037/ a0023304.

18   Manning, Rachel, Mark Levine, and Alan Collins. 2007. "The Kitty Genovese Murder and the Social Psychology of Helping: The Parable of the 38 Witnesses." *American Psychologist* 62 (6): 555–62. doi:10.1037/0003-066X.62.6.555.

19   Jensen, Jessica, and Steven Thompson. 2016. "The Incident Command System: A Literature Review." *Disasters* 40 (1): 158–82. doi:10.1111/disa.12135.

20   Griggs, John Wyeth. "BP Gulf of Mexico Oil Spill." *Energy* LJ 32 (2011): 57.

21   Smith, Gerry. 2013. "Don't Count on Your Cell Phone for Help After the Next Huge Hurricane." *Huffington Post UK.* https://www.huffpost.com/entry/cell-phones-hurricane -sandy.

22   Kabel, Allison, and Catherine Chmidling. 2014. "Disaster Prepper: Health, Identity, and American Survivalist Culture." *Human Organization* 73 (3): 258-266. doi:10.17730/ humo.73.3.l34252tg03428527.

23   The Collected Wisdom of Banacek. 2010. YouTube video. https://www.youtube.com /watch?v=ykuGCT2uixk&t=1s.

24   Henderson, T. L., K. A. Roberto, and Y. Kamo. 2010. "Older Adults' Responses to Hurricane Katrina: Daily Hassles and Coping Strategies." *Journal of Applied Gerontology* 29 (1): 48–69. doi:10.1177/0733464809334287.

25   McMillan, Carl. "The ABCs, Ds, and Ks of Fire Extinguishers." *Occupational Health and Safety* 73, no. 8 (2004): 42–44.

26   Insider, Business. 2017. "Scientists Once Nuked Beer to See If It'd Still Be Drinkable After an Atomic Blast." ScienceAlert. https://www.sciencealert.com/scientists-once-nuked-beers -to-see-if-they-d-still-be-drinkable-after-an-atomic-blast.

27   Holland, Dean, dir. "Emergency Response." *Parks and Recreation*, season 5, episode 13, National Broadcasting Company (NBC), 2013.

28   Hortensius, Ruud, Dennis J. L. G. Schutter, and Beatrice de Gelder. 2016. "Personal Distress and the Influence of Bystanders on Responding to an Emergency." *Cognitive, Affective, & Behavioral Neuroscience* 16 (4): 672–688. doi:10.3758/s13415-016-0423-6.

29   Centers of Disease Control. 2019. "CERC: Psychology of a Crisis." 2019 update: US
     Human and Health Services.

30   "Surveillance for Illness and Injury After Hurricane Katrina—Three Counties, Mississippi,
     September 5–October 11, 2005." 2006. MMWR-CDC. https://www.cdc.gov/mmwr
     /preview/mmwrhtml/mm5509a2.htm.

31   "In Katrina's Wake." 2022. National Library of Medicine. https://www.ncbi.nlm.nih.gov
     /pmc/articles/PMC1332683/#:~:text=In%20coordination%20with%20the%20Louisiana
     ,%2C%20herbicides%2C%20and%20polychlorinated%20biphenyls.

32   Schildkraut, Jaclyn, and Glenn W. Muschert. 2019. "Columbine, 20 Years Later and
     Beyond: Lessons from Tragedy."

33   Cutler, Nancy. 2022. "Deaths From 9/11 Diseases Will Soon Outnumber Those Lost on
     that Fateful Day." *USA Today*. https://www.usatoday.com/story/news/nation-now/2018/09
     /06/9-11-deaths-aftermath-soon-outnumber-killed-sept-11/1209605002/.

34   Walsh, Froma. 2007. "Traumatic Loss and Major Disasters: Strengthening Family
     and Community Resilience." *Family Process* 46 (2): 207–227. doi:10.1111/j.1545-
     5300.2007.00205.x.

35   "Disaster Distress Helpline." 2012. SAMHSA. https://www.samhsa.gov/find-help/disaster
     -distress-helpline.

36   "CPR Steps." 2022. American Red Cross. https://www.redcross.org/take-a-class/cpr
     /performing-cpr/cpr-steps.

37   Family Advisory Board of the Transitions ACR. 2019. "For Families or Caregivers: Self-
     Care is Putting on YOUR Oxygen Mask First." Worcester, MA: University of Massachusetts
     Medical School, Department of Psychiatry, Implementation Science and Practice Advances
     Research Center (iSPARC), Transitions to Adulthood Center for Research.

38   "Immediately Dangerous to Life or Health (IDLH) Values." 2019. IDLH Values. https://
     www.cdc.gov/niosh/idlh/default.html.

39   Spaaij, R., and M. S. Hamm. 2015. "Endgame? Sports Events as Symbolic Targets in Lone
     Wolf Terrorism." *Studies in Conflict & Terrorism* 38 (12), 1022–1037. https://doi.org/10.1
     080/1057610X.2015.1076695.

40   Watkins, Ali, Michael Rothfeld, William Rashbaum, and Brian Rosenthal. 2020. "Top
     E.R. Doctor Who Treated Virus Patients Dies by Suicide." *New York Times*. https://www.
     nytimes.com/2020/04/27/nyregion/new-york-city-doctor-suicide-coronavirus.html.

41   Garstang, M., and M. Kelley. 2017. "Understanding Animal Detection of Precursor
     Earthquake Sounds." *Animals* 7 (12), 66.

42   Adnan, A., M. Z. Ramli, and S. M. Razak. 2015. "Disaster Management and Mitigation
     For Earthquakes: Are We Ready?" *9th Asia Pacific Structural Engineering and Construction
     Conference* (APSEC2015).

43   Teaganne, Finn. 2022. "Biden Warns Americans in Ukraine to Leave, Says Sending Troops
     to Evacuate Would Be 'World War.'" NBC News. https://www.nbcnews.com/politics/white
     -house/biden-warns-americans-leave-ukraine-russia-troops-world-war-rcna15781.

44   Lee, Bruce. *Tao of Jeet Kun Do*. Ohara Publications: Burbank, California, 1975.

45   Holweg, E. J. 2000. "Mariner's Guide for Hurricane Awareness in the North Atlantic
     Basin."

46 Rosenthal, M. Sara. 2013. "The End-of-Life Experiences of 9/11 Civilians: Death and Dying in the World Trade Center." *OMEGA—Journal of Death and Dying* 67 (4): 329–361. doi:10.2190/om.67.4.a.

47 Thompson, Andrea. 2018. "Why Did Hurricane Michael Rev Up to Cateogry 4 So Quickly?" *Scientific American*. https://www.scientificamerican.com/article/why-did-hurricane-michael-rev-up-to-category-4-so-quickly/.

48 Halverson, Jeffrey B. 2014. "A Mighty Wind: The Derecho of June 29, 2012." *Weatherwise* 67 (4): 24–31. doi:10.1080/00431672.2014.918788.

49 Jacobellis v. Ohio. 1964 378 U.S. 184. US Supreme Court.

50 "A Volcanic Trip—With the Lord of the Rings." 2010. *Chess News*. https://en.chessbase.com/post/a-volcanic-trip-with-the-lord-of-the-rings.

51 Kwasinski, Alexis, Fabio Andrade, Marcel J. Castro-Sitiriche, and Efrain O'Neill-Carrillo. 2019. "Hurricane Maria Effects on Puerto Rico Electric Power Infrastructure." *IEEE Power and Energy Technology Systems Journal* 6 (1): 85–94. doi:10.1109/jpets.2019.2900293.

52 "Florida Sign Language Interpreter Hired to Warn Residents of Hurricane Just Sort of Wings It." 2022. *GQ*. https://www.gq.com/story/florida-sign-language-bear-monster.

53 World Economic Forum. 2018. "Digital Identity Threshold, Digital Identity Revolution." https://www3.weforum.org/docs/White_Paper_Digital_Identity_Threshold_Digital_Identity_Revolution_report_2018.pdf.

54 Meltani, Megan. 2017. "Harvey Evacuees Leave Their Belongings—and Health Records—Behind." *WIRED*. https://www.wired.com/story/harvey-evacuees-leave-their-belongings-and-health-records-behind/.

55 "Falsely Padding Deductions Highlighted in IRS 2018 'Dirty Dozen' Tax Scams." 2018. Internal Revenue Service. https://www.irs.gov/newsroom/falsely-padding-deductions-highlighted-in-irs-2018-dirty-dozen-tax-scams.

56 Feeney-Hart, Alison. 2013. "The Little-Told Story of the Massive WWII Pet Cull." BBC News. https://www.bbc.com/news/magazine-24478532.

57 Kahn, Christopher, E. Brooke Lerner, and David Cone. 2010. "Triage." *Disaster Medicine*. 1st ed., 175. Cambridge: Cambridge University Press.

58 Ibid.

59 Ackerman, Andy, dir. "The Nap." *Seinfeld*, season 8, episode 18, National Broadcasting Company (NBC), 1997.

60 Johnson, Jon. 2019. "How Long Can You Live Without Water? Facts and Effects." *Medical News Today*. https://www.medicalnewstoday.com/articles/325174.

61 Smith, Andy. 1984. "Andy Smith to President Ronald Regan." Reagan Library.

62 Levenson, Thomas. 2020. "The Truth About Isaac Newton's Productive Plague." *The New Yorker*. https://www.newyorker.com/culture/cultural-comment/the-truth-about-isaac-newtons-productive-plague.

63 Marshall, Jennifer, Jacqueline Wiltshire, Jennifer Delva, Temitope Bello, and Anthony J. Masys. 2020. "Natural and Manmade Disasters: Vulnerable Populations." *Advanced Sciences and Technologies For Security Applications* 143–161. doi:10.1007/978-3-030-23491-1_7.

64 Kayyem, Juliette N. 2022. *The Devil Never Sleeps: Learning to Live in the Age of Disasters.* 1st ed. New York: Perseus Books.

65 Alexander, M. E., and M. G. Cruz. 2012. "Modelling the Effects of Surface and Crown Fire Behaviour on Serotinous Cone Opening in Jack Pine and Lodgepole Pine Forests." *International Journal of Wildland Fire* 21 (6): 709. doi:10.1071/wf11153.

66 Furtado, Shandra. 2022. "The Important Relationship Between Forests and Fire." *American Forests.* https://www.americanforests.org/article/the-important-relationship-between-forests -and-fire.

67 *Garry Kasparov Teaches Chess.* 2020. DVD. Masterclass.

68 Ibid.

69 "Your COVID." 2020. *Wall Street Journal.* May 2020. p.A7.

70 Scott, Ryan. 2014. "Will Your Business Recover from Disaster?" *Forbes.* https://www .forbes.com/sites/causeintegration/2014/09/04/will-your-business-recover-from-disaster/.

71 Levenson, Thomas. 2020. "The Truth About Isaac Newton's Productive Plague." *The New Yorker.* https://www.newyorker.com/culture/cultural-comment/the-truth-about-isaac -newtons-productive-plague.

72 "Bank of America: The Humble Beginnings of a Large Bank." 2022. Office of the Comptroller of the Currency. https://www.occ.treas.gov/about/who-we-are/history/1866 -1913/1866-1913-bank-of-america.html.

73 Campbell, Mark. 2020. "What Are the Consequences of Data Loss?" Unitrends. https:// www.unitrends.com/blog/what-are-the-consequences-of-data-loss.

74 Cucinotta, Domenico, and Maurizio Vanelli. 2020. "WHO Declares COVID-19 a Pandemic." *Acta Bio-Medica: Atenei Parmensis* vol. 91, 1 157–160. doi:10.23750/abm. v91i1.9397.

75 Bell, Gavin A., and W. Stacy Miller II. 2021. "Fraud in the Pandemic: How COVID-19 Affects Qui Tam Whistleblowers and the False Claims Act." *Campbell Law Review* 43: 273.

76 Maze, Jonathan. 2021. "Why Domino's Gave Out Gift Cards to Local Restaurants." *Restaurant Business.* https://www.restaurantbusinessonline.com/marketing/why-dominos -gave-out-gift-cards-local-restaurants.

77 Thoreau, Henry David. *The Journal, 1837–1861.* Ed. Damien Searls. NYRB Classics: New York, 2011.

78 Kurniawan, Lilik, Soesilo Zauhar, Syamsul Maarif, and Lely Indah Mindarti. 2022. "Strengthening Community Resilience at Balerante Village, Klaten Regency, Central Java Province (Study Case: Merapi Volcano Hazard)." *Journal of Management Information and Decision Sciences* 25 (3): 1, 2.

INDEX

ABOUT THE AUTHOR

Patrick Hardy is founder and CEO of Hytropy Disaster Management, the largest full-service small business and family disaster management company in the US. A Certified Emergency Manager, Master Business Continuity Professional, Certified Risk Manager, and FEMA Master of Exercise Practitioner, he has extensive experience working in the public, private, and nonprofit sectors in disaster management from micro-businesses to Fortune 500 companies such as Google, Merck, and Parsons Corporation.

In the summer of 2012, he became the youngest person and the first micro-business owner ever to be selected as the National Private Sector Representative to the Federal Emergency Management Agency (FEMA) in Washington, DC, designing a small business disaster framework.

Patrick is considered the world's leading expert in small business and family disaster preparedness, having worked with tens of thousands of organizations and families (including high-net-worth family offices). He has been published in dozens of industry journals and periodicals, as well as popular media outlets such as *Today* and *Yahoo!*. He has been a featured expert on family disaster preparedness on *Good Morning America, PA Live!,* and NBC and CBS affiliates throughout the US.

At the height of the COVID-19 pandemic, Patrick launched Disaster Hawk®, the first mobile app for families and small businesses to create fully customizable disaster plans for natural, technological, and security emergencies, including COVID-19. Patrick is a decorated, award-winning international public speaker who presents to organizations worldwide, and is one of fewer than ninety-five people to earn Toastmasters' Accredited Speaker designation.

Patrick is the first small business expert to be appointed as the National Sector Chief for Commercial Facilities for InfraGard, the FBI's public–private partnership. He is also the first small business board member to sit on the US chapter of the ARISE Global network, established by the United Nations Office for Disaster Risk Reduction (UNDRR).

A longtime volunteer to the American Red Cross and other disaster non-profits, he has worked in sheltering, emergency response, and the Emergency Operations Center. He has been cross-trained and certified in hazmat, emergency communications, homeland security policy, and terrorism. Patrick began his career in EMS ambulance first response, eventually becoming a visiting instructor to the National EMS Academy's paramedic program, and wrote the chapters on disaster preparedness, terrorism, and weapons of mass destruction for the *Advanced Emergency Medical Technician Textbook*.